GRAMMAR *EXPRESS* BASIC

WORKBOOK

Marjorie Fuchs | **Margaret Bonner**

Longman

Grammar Express Basic Workbook

Pearson Education, 10 Bank Street, White Plains, NY 10606

Executive editor: Laura Le Dréan
Senior production editor: Robert Ruvo
Marketing manager: Joe Chapple
Director of manufacturing: Patrice Fraccio
Senior manufacturing buyer: Edith Pullman
Photo research: Dana Klinek
Cover design adaptation: Pat Wosczyk
Text design: Pat Wosczyk
Associate digital layout manager: Paula D. Williams
Text font: New Century Schoolbook 10.5/12
Illustrations: **Chris Gash:** pp. 65, 81; **Peter Grau:** pp. 7, 116; **Jock MacRae:** pp. 49, 68;
   Paul McCusker: pp. 8, 31, 57, 115; **Andy Myer:** p. 55; **Dusan Petricic:** p. 17
Photo credits: **Page 3,** © RubberBall Productions. **Page 26,** © Bettmann/CORBIS.
   Page 72, © Ryan McVay/Photodisc/Getty Images. **Page 76,** left: © Photodisc/Getty Images.
   right: © Bernard Annebicque/CORBIS SYGMA. **Page 78,** © David Young-Wolff/Photo Edit.
   Page 83, AP/Wide World Photos. **Page 97,** © Wolfgang Kaehler/CORBIS.

ISBN: 0-13-184926-3

Printed in the United States of America
5 6 7 8 9 10–CRK–08

Contents

To The Student

Dear Student,

The **Grammar Express Basic Workbook** will give you more practice in all the grammar points that you are studying in **Grammar Express Basic**. The **Workbook** is easy to use:

Organization

- There are 50 units, the same number as in **Grammar Express Basic**.
- The number of each **Workbook** unit is the same as the number of the unit in **Grammar Express Basic**.
- Each **Workbook** unit is two pages long.
- Each **Workbook** unit has three to five exercises.
- The **Workbook** unit practices the same grammar as the **Grammar Express Basic** unit.
- Like **Grammar Express Basic**, the **Workbook** has twelve parts with a SelfTest after each part.

Exercises

- The first exercise of each unit often practices the form of the grammar.
- The other exercises practice the grammar in sentences and short paragraphs.
- There are many exercise types: multiple choice, fill-in-the-blanks, chart completion, matching, putting words in the correct order, editing (finding and correcting errors), and asking and answering questions. You will also practice spelling and contractions.
- Most of the exercises are similar to the ones in **Grammar Express Basic**. You won't have to learn a lot of new exercise types or instructions.

SelfTests

- There is a SelfTest after each part. The SelfTest tests the grammar from all the units in that part.
- The questions are similar to the ones on the TOEFL test.

Checking Your Work

- You can check your answers in the **Answer Key** at the back of the book.

- Most of the exercises have just one answer so you can see right away if your answer is correct.

How to Use This Workbook

- After you complete a **Grammar Express Basic** unit, do the **Workbook** exercises for that unit.

- Check your answers in the **Workbook Answer Key**.

- If you make a lot of mistakes, review the first two pages in the **Grammar Express Basic** unit. (The Grammar Charts and The Grammar Explanations and Examples)

- Try the **Workbook** exercises again! (You can use a separate piece of paper).

- When you finish a part, do the SelfTest to check your progress.

You can use the **Workbook** in school or on your own. In class or at home for self-study, we think you will enjoy using the **Grammar Express Basic Workbook!**

With best wishes for success in your English studies,

Marjorie Fuchs and Margaret Bonner

The Present of *Be*:
Statements

1 | **CONTRACTIONS** • *Rewrite these sentences. Use contractions.*

1. She is a dancer.   <u>She's a dancer.</u>

2. They are not here.   _____ OR _____

3. We are from Turkey.   _____

4. He is not a student.   _____ OR _____

5. It is a good class.   _____

6. There is a computer on the desk.   _____

7. I am twenty-one years old.   _____

8. You are a good friend.   _____

9. I am not tall.   _____

10. She is not at the library.   _____ OR _____

2 | **AFFIRMATIVE STATEMENTS** • *Complete the sentences.*

1. My name ___<u>is</u>___ Carlos. ___<u>I'm</u>___ Spanish.

2. Her name _____ Leyla. _____ from Turkey.

3. Hi! _____ Olga. This _____ Peter. _____ students.

4. Our teacher _____ Mr. Miller. _____ from Canada.

5. Peter and I _____ good friends.

6. Peter and Olga _____ friends too.

7. They _____ interested in music.

8. I _____ interested in music too.

3 | **THERE IS *OR* THERE ARE** • *Complete the sentences with* **there is** *or* **there are**.

1. ___<u>There are</u>___ twenty students in my class.

2. _____ five students from Brazil.

3. _____ one student from China.

4. _____ four computers in the class.

5. _____ a big clock on the wall.

6. _____ a large window.

7. _____ thirty desks.

8. _____ a lot of books on the desks.

4 **NEGATIVE STATEMENTS** • *Write negative sentences. Use contractions.*

1. Maria is from Colombia. Alvaro ___isn't from Colombia.___

2. She's a student. He _____

3. They're interested in sports. Jason and Ana _____

4. Jason and Ana are friends. Jason and I _____

5. Ms. Gordon is an English teacher. I _____

6. She's interested in baseball. Her students _____

7. I'm an English student. You _____

8. Ms. Gordon is from Australia. We _____

5 **AFFIRMATIVE AND NEGATIVE STATEMENTS** • *Complete the sentences.*

<table>
<tr>
<td>

**Canadian Language Institute
Student ID**

Name: Renata   Petrov
         (first)   (last)
Country: Russia
Class: English 101

</td>
<td>

**Canadian Language Institute
Student ID**

Name: Bao   Tran
         (first)   (last)
Country: Vietnam
Class: English 102

</td>
</tr>
</table>

1. Her first name __isn't__ Petrov. It _____ Renata.

2. She _____ a teacher. She _____ a student.

3. She _____ from Russia.

4. His first name _____ Bao. It _____ Tran.

5. He _____ from Russia. He _____ from Vietnam.

6. Renata and Bao _____ in the same school.

7. Renata _____ in English 101.

8. Bao and Renata _____ in the same class.

9. The school _____ the Canadian Language Institute.

10. It _____ in the United States. It _____ in Canada.

11. I _____ a student at the Canadian Language Institute.

12. We _____ in Renata's class.

UNIT 2

The Present of *Be*:
Questions

---

1 **YES/NO QUESTIONS** • *Read these sentences. Ask questions about the words in parentheses.*

1. Teresa is here.

(Jason) _____Is Jason here?_____

2. My friends are at the library.

(your friends) _____

3. They're afraid of dogs.

(you) _____

4. He's a doctor.

(she) _____

5. Daniel is late.

(I) _____

6. My sister is right.

(we) _____

7. Ana's from Mexico.

(they) _____

8. She's a student.

(he) _____

9. He's OK.

(you) _____

10. He's here.

(she) _____

2 **SHORT ANSWERS** • *Look at the chart. Answer the questions. Use contractions when possible.*

NAME	COUNTRY	OCCUPATION
Men:		
Javier	Brazil	teacher
Klaus	Germany	photographer
Vadim	Turkey	student
Women:		
Irena	Russia	computer programmer
Soo-Min	Korea	doctor
Marta	Mexico	student

1. Is Marta from Mexico? _____Yes, she is._____

2. Is Irena from Brazil? _____

3. Are Klaus and Soo-Min students? _____

4. Is Javier a teacher? _____

5. Is he from Portugal? _____

6. Are Klaus and Irena from Austria? _____

Now answer these questions.

7. Are you a student? _____

8. Are you and your classmates English teachers? _____

3 **WH- QUESTIONS AND ANSWERS •** *Write questions. Answer these questions with your own information.*

1. Q: _____What is your name?_____ (What / your / name)

   A: _____

2. Q: _____ (Where / you / from)

   A: _____

3. Q: _____ (Who / your / teacher)

   A: _____

4. Q: _____ (What / your hobbies)

   A: _____

5. Q: _____ (What / you / afraid of)

   A: _____

4 **QUESTIONS AND ANSWERS •** *Complete the conversations with* **am**, **is**, *or* **are** *and short answers. Use contractions when possible.*

1. **A:** Hi, Maria. How _____are_____ you?
     a.

   B: Fine, thanks. _____ I late?
                        b.

   A: _____. You're early!
          c.

2. **A:** _____ you OK?
          a.

   B: _____. I'm sick.
          b.

   A: Oh, sorry! Speak to Sara.

   B: Sara? _____ a doctor?
                 c.

   A: _____. She's a great doctor. Call her!
          d.

3. **A:** What _____ your apartment number?
              a.

   B: 24-H.

   A: _____ it on the 24th floor?
          b.

   B: _____. Why? _____ you afraid of high places?
          c.   **d.**

   A: _____. My apartment is on the 24th floor too!
          e.

UNIT 3

The Present Progressive:
Statements

---

1 **SPELLING** • *Add* **-ing** *to these verbs. Make all necessary spelling changes.*

1. talk _____talking_____
2. call _____
3. leave _____
4. play _____
5. sit _____

6. have _____
7. get _____
8. run _____
9. work _____
10. come _____

2 **CONTRACTIONS** • *Rewrite these sentences. Use contractions.*

1. He is working _____He's working._____
2. We are talking on the phone. _____
3. They are not listening. _____ OR _____
4. She is taking the train. _____
5. I am not reading. _____
6. You are speaking very loud. _____
7. He is not sleeping. _____ OR _____

3 **AFFIRMATIVE STATEMENTS** • *Complete the sentences with the present progressive form of the verbs in parentheses.*

1. Antonio _____is working_____ today.
   (work)
2. He _____ on the phone.
   (talk)
3. His friends _____ at the library.
   (study)
4. Paulo _____ a book about trains.
   (read)
5. I _____ too.
   (study)
6. We _____ outside.
   (sit)
7. My classmates and I _____ exercises.
   (do)
8. It _____ hard.
   (rain)
9. I _____ wet.
   (get)
10. My friends _____ now.
    (leave)

4 **NEGATIVE STATEMENTS** • *Write negative sentences. Use contractions.*

1. My brother is working. My sister _____isn't working_____.

2. He's studying at home. He _____ at the library.

3. Our friends are leaving. Our parents _____.

4. I'm calling my sister. I _____ my brother.

5. She's taking the train. She _____ the bus.

6. Doug is drinking coffee. He _____ tea.

7. You're listening to me. She _____ to me.

8. This train is going to Paris. It _____ to Lyon.

5 **AFFIRMATIVE AND NEGATIVE STATEMENTS** • *Look at the picture. Complete the sentences with the present progressive form of the verbs in parentheses. Use the affirmative or negative.*

1. Sara _____isn't driving_____ to work today.
   (drive)

2. She _____ the train.
   (take)

3. It _____.
   (rain)

4. Sara and her friend _____.
   (talk)

5. A man _____ across from them.
   (sit)

6. He _____.
   (sleep)

7. He _____ to the two women.
   (speak)

8. He _____ on his cell phone.
   (talk)

9. The women _____ to his conversation.
   (listen)

10. They _____ their conversation.
    (enjoy)

The Present Progressive:
Questions

1   **YES/NO QUESTIONS AND SHORT ANSWERS** • *Look at the picture. Write questions with the words in parentheses and write short answers.*

1. **Q:** Is the man watching TV?   (the man / watch TV)
   A: No, he isn't.

2. **Q:** _____ (the woman / talk on the phone)
   A: _____

3. **Q:** _____ (she / read)
   A: _____

4. **Q:** _____ (she / read / a book)
   A: _____

5. **Q:** _____ (it / rain)
   A: _____

6. **Q:** _____ (the children / watch TV)
   A: _____

7. **Q:** _____ (they / play)
   A: _____

8. **Q:** _____ (the cat / sleep)
   A: _____

2   **WH- QUESTIONS AND ANSWERS** • *Ask and answer questions about the picture in Exercise 1.*

1. **Q:** Who's talking on the phone?
             (Who / talk on the phone)
   A: The man.

2. **Q:** _____
             (What / Ana / read)
   A: _____

3. **Q:** _____
             (What / the cat / do)
   A: _____

4. **Q:** _____
             (Where / the cat / sleep)
   A: _____

8

5. **Q:** _____
   (Why / the cat / sleep)

   A: _____

6. **Q:** _____
   (What / the children / do)

   A: _____

3 **QUESTIONS AND ANSWERS • Complete the conversations with the present progressive form of the verbs in parentheses and with short answers.**

1. **A:** Hi. What ____are____ you ____doing____?
           a. (do)

   B: I'm trying to sleep, but I can't.

   A: Why not? _____ you _____ about something?
                              b. (worry)

   B: _____. My math test. It's tomorrow.
          c.

2. **A:** What _____ you _____?
                          a. (watch)

   B: The weather channel.

   A: What _____ they _____? Is it going to snow?
                          b. (say)

   B: _____. It's going to start soon.
          c.

3. **A:** _____ it _____ in Greenville?
                      a. (snow)

   B: _____. The sun is shining.
          b.

4. **A:** Why _____ you _____ out the window?
                          a. (look)

   _____ it_____?
              b. (snow)

   B: _____. And it's beautiful. Come and see.
          c.

   A: I can't. I'm busy.

   B: What _____ you _____?
                          d. (do)

   A: I'm studying for my math test.

5. **A:** Who _____ you _____ to?
                          a. (talk)

   B: It's Sara. She's calling from the train station.

   A: _____ she _____ Tom's train?
                      b. (meet)

   B: _____. It's arriving now.
          c.

   A: _____ Tom _____ alone?
                      d. (come)

   B: _____. His roommate is with him.
          e.

SelfTest

Circle the letter of the correct answer to complete each sentence.

EXAMPLE: Carlos _____ a student.　　　　　　　　　　**A B (C) D**
　　　(A) are　　　　　　　(C) is
　　　(B) does　　　　　　 (D) were

1. Andy's hobbies _____ photography and sports.　　**A B C D**
　　(A) are　　　　　　　(C) be
　　(B) is　　　　　　　 (D) being

2. He's _____ English now.　　　　　　　　　　　　**A B C D**
　　(A) study　　　　　　(C) studying
　　(B) studies　　　　　 (D) is studying

3. _____ late?　　　　　　　　　　　　　　　　　　**A B C D**
　　(A) I am　　　　　　　(C) Did I
　　(B) Am I　　　　　　　(D) I

4. _____ you talking on the phone?　　　　　　　　**A B C D**
　　(A) Is　　　　　　　　(C) Are
　　(B) Why　　　　　　　 (D) Do

5. Carlos _____ a shower right now.　　　　　　　　**A B C D**
　　(A) taking　　　　　　(C) is taking
　　(B) takes　　　　　　 (D) are taking

6. _____ Tania?　　　　　　　　　　　　　　　　　**A B C D**
　　(A) Where　　　　　　(C) Is where
　　(B) Where is　　　　　(D) Where she

7. They're _____ in the same class.　　　　　　　　**A B C D**
　　(A) no　　　　　　　　(C) don't
　　(B) aren't　　　　　　(D) not

8. Where _____ going?　　　　　　　　　　　　　　**A B C D**
　　(A) are you　　　　　　(C) you
　　(B) you are　　　　　　(D) is you

9. _____ are watching a movie.　　　　　　　　　　**A B C D**
　　(A) I　　　　　　　　　(C) We
　　(B) He　　　　　　　　(D) Who

10. —Are you busy right now?　　　　　　　　　　　　　**A B C D**
　　 —Yes, I _____. Sorry.
　　(A) am　　　　　　　　(C) 'm not
　　(B) 'm　　　　　　　　(D) is

11. _____ are some good restaurants near school.　**A B C D**
　　(A) Where　　　　　　(C) They're
　　(B) This　　　　　　　(D) There

12. —Is Tom traveling with you?
    —No, he _____.
    (A) not   (C) not travel
    (B) 's not   (D) 're not

A B C D

SECTION TWO

Each sentence has four underlined parts. The four underlined parts are marked A, B, C, and D. Circle the letter of the part that is NOT CORRECT.

EXAMPLE:

Carla <u>is</u> a student, but she <u>are</u> <u>not</u> in school <u>today</u>.
   A   B   C   D

A (B) C D

13. Tania <u>is</u> <u>have</u> lunch in the cafeteria <u>now</u>, and Tom <u>is</u> in class.
    A B   C   D

A B C D

14. I <u>amn't</u> <u>studying</u> <u>now</u>, but I'm <u>sitting</u> in the library.
     A   B   C   D

A B C D

15. The coffee <u>is</u> strong, so we'<u>re</u> <u>drink</u> tea <u>today</u>.
         A   B C   D

A B C D

16. <u>There</u> <u>is</u> a bank near school, but <u>they</u> is <u>not</u> open today.
   A   B   C   D

A B C D

17. <u>Why</u> <u>you</u> <u>are</u> at home <u>now</u>?
   A   B   C D

A B C D

18. He <u>no is</u> <u>driving</u> because his sister <u>is</u> <u>using</u> his car today.
     A   B   C D

A B C D

19. <u>What</u> <u>they are</u> reading in their English <u>class</u>?
   A   B   C D

A B C D

20. Sally <u>is</u> <u>reading</u>, and her roommate <u>are</u> <u>listening</u> to music.
      A   B   C   D

A B C D

21. <u>Lea</u> <u>is</u> your <u>sister</u>, or <u>is</u> <u>she</u> your cousin?
   A   B   C D

A B C D

22. Where <u>are</u> <u>you</u> <u>going</u> <u>now.</u>
       A   B C   D

A B C D

23. Mike <u>drinks</u> soda, but Pete <u>is</u> <u>having</u> coffee with <u>lunch.</u>
     A   B C   D

A B C D

24. <u>They</u> <u>is</u> a good movie in town, but we'<u>re</u> busy <u>tonight</u>.
   A B   C   D

A B C D

25. Darla and Ian <u>are</u> <u>not</u> <u>working</u> today, so <u>they's</u> at the beach.
            A B   C   D

A B C D

The Simple Present:
Statements

1   **SPELLING • Complete with the correct form of the verb.**

I	HE / SHE / IT		I	HE / SHE / IT
1. drink	drinks	**6.**	don't	_____
2. have	_____	**7.**	take	_____
3. watch	_____	**8.**	do	_____
4. go	_____	**9.**	am	_____
5. work	_____	**10.**	relax	_____

2   **AFFIRMATIVE STATEMENTS • Complete the sentences with the simple present form of the verbs in the parentheses.**

1. Shao-fen _____lives_____ in Taiwan.
   (live)
2. She and her sister _____ to the same school.
   (go)
3. They _____ music.
   (study)
4. After school, Shao-fen _____ home.
   (go)
5. Her sister often _____ in school.
   (stay)
6. She _____ a piano lesson every Wednesday.
   (have)
7. The two sisters always _____ dinner with their family.
   (have)
8. Their parents always _____ with them.
   (eat)
9. After dinner, Shao-fen usually _____ the dishes.
   (wash)
10. Her sister _____ homework.
    (do)
11. Their parents _____.
    (read)
12. Shao-fen always _____ in front of the TV.
    (relax)

3   **TIME WORDS • Put these words in the correct order.**

1. never • drinks • coffee • Sara _____Sara never drinks coffee._____
2. makes • It • her • always • nervous _____
3. drinks • tea • She • usually _____

4. She • adds • sometimes • milk and sugar _____

5. Tomás • drives • to work • usually _____

6. sometimes • He • the bus • takes _____

7. on time • He • always • is _____

8. never • He • is • late _____

4 ***NEGATIVE STATEMENTS* • *Write negative sentences. Use contractions.***

1. Sara drinks tea. Dan _____ *doesn't drink tea.* _____

2. Coffee makes Sara nervous. Tea _____

3. Dan works in an office. Sara _____

4. Sara goes to school. Dan _____

5. Sara's parents live in the city. Dan's parents _____

6. Sara and Dan speak English. Their parents _____

7. Dan likes computer games. Sara _____

8. Sara plays tennis. Dan _____

9. Sara lives near Dan. I _____

10. They go to the movies together. We _____

5 ***AFFIRMATIVE AND NEGATIVE STATEMENTS* • *Look at Tomás's schedule. Complete the sentences with the correct form of the verbs in parentheses.***

1. Tomás ___*doesn't get*___ up at 7:00.
   (get)

2. He _____ up at 7:30.
   (get)

3. He _____ breakfast at 8:00.
   (have)

4. He _____ the train to work.
   (take)

5. He and Jorge _____ at 8:00.
   (meet)

6. They always _____ for two hours.
   (meet)

7. Tomás _____ e-mail before lunch.
   (answer)

8. He _____ lunch at his meetings.
   (have)

9. He _____ reports after lunch.
   (write)

10. Ana _____ with him at 2:00.
    (meet)

11. They _____ with Jorge.
    (meet)

12. Tomás _____ phone calls before 5:00.
    (make)

DAILY SCHEDULE	
7:30 get up	12:00–1:00 lunch
8:00 breakfast	1:00–2:00 write reports
8:30 drive to work	2:00–4:00 meeting with Ana
9:00–11:00 meeting with Jorge	4:00–5:00 phone calls
11:00–12:00 answer e-mail	5:00 drive home

The Simple Present:
Questions

1 **YES/NO QUESTIONS** • *Read these sentences. Ask questions.*

1. Silvio smiles a lot. What about Lia?

   _Does Lia smile a lot?_____

2. My club meets every week. What about her club?

   _____

3. She tells a lot of jokes. What about Silvio?

   _____

4. Silvio speaks Portuguese. What about Lia?

   _____

5. Silvio is very funny. What about Lia?

   _____

6. Silvio's friends laugh a lot. What about Lia's friends?

   _____

7. I laugh a lot. What about you?

   _____

8. My club meets in the park. What about your club?

   _____

2 **YES/NO QUESTIONS AND SHORT ANSWERS** • *Complete the questions with the correct form of the verbs in parentheses and write short answers.*

1. A: _____Do_____ you ___speak___ Spanish?

                   a. (speak)

   B: _No, I don't_. I speak English and Portuguese.

    b.

2. A: _____ Paulo _____ Portuguese?

                  a. (speak)

   B: _____. Portuguese is his first language.

    b.

3. A: _____ your friends _____ a lot?

                  a. (study)

   B: _____. They study all the time.

    b.

4. A: _____ you _____ to a club?

                  a. (belong)

   B: _____. I belong to an English club.

    b.

14

5. **A:** _____ your club _____ on Monday?
   a. (meet)
   B: _____. It meets on Tuesday.
   b.

6. **A:** _____ you _____ in the park?
   a. (meet)
   B: _____. We meet at my house.
   b.

7. **A:** _____ your club _____ a lot?
   a. (cost)
   B: _____. It's free.
   b.

8. **A:** _____ you _____ English?
   a. (speak)
   B: _____. I speak English and Chinese.
   b.

9. **A:** _____ you and your classmates _____ the club?
   a. (enjoy)
   B: _____. It's fun!
   b.

3 **WH- QUESTIONS** • *Read the answers. Then ask questions about the underlined words.*

1. **Q:** *Where do they meet?* _____
   A: They meet <u>in the park</u>.

2. **Q:** _____
   A: They have class <u>once a week</u>.

3. **Q:** _____
   A: They meet <u>on Friday</u>.

4. **Q:** _____
   A: She feels <u>very comfortable</u>.

5. **Q:** _____
   A: She wears <u>jeans</u>.

6. **Q:** _____
   A: A movie ticket costs <u>$5</u>.

7. **Q:** _____
   A: He likes <u>his teacher</u>.

8. **Q:** _____
   A: She studies every day <u>because she wants to get good grades</u>.

9. **Q:** _____
   A: She does her homework <u>at the library</u>.

10. **Q:** _____
    A: She goes home <u>at 5:00</u>.

UNIT 7 — Non-Action Verbs

1 **ACTION OR NON-ACTION** • *Circle the correct words.*

1. **A:** It ('s)/ 's being a beautiful day.
      a.

   B: Do / Are you want / wanting to go for a walk?
        b.   **c.**

2. **A:** What do / are you do / doing?
            a.   **b.**

   B: I look / 'm looking for my umbrella. Do / Are you see / seeing it?
          c.   **d.**   **e.**

3. **A:** I 'm / 'm being hungry.
          a.

   B: Do / Are you want / wanting to make dinner?
        b.   **c.**

4. **A:** What do / are you cook / cooking? It smells / 's smelling great.
            a.   **b.**   **c.**

   B: Spaghetti sauce. Do / Are you want / wanting to taste it?
                    d.   **e.**

   A: Mmmm. It tastes / 's tasting good.
              f.

5. **A:** Do / Are we have / having any garlic? I need / 'm needing it for the sauce.
        a.   **b.**   **c.**

   B: I think / 'm thinking there's some in the refrigerator.
          d.

6. **A:** Do / Are you like / liking the sauce?
        a.   **b.**

   B: I love / 'm loving it! I want / 'm wanting the recipe.
          c.   **d.**

7. **A:** What do / are you listen / listening to?
            a.   **b.**

   B: My new CD.

   A: It sounds / 's sounding great. Who sings / 's singing?
              c.   **d.**

   B: The Dragons. They 're / are being from England.
                        e.

8. **A:** I go / 'm going to the store. Do / Are we need / needing anything?
          a.   **b.**   **c.**

   B: Yes. Garlic.

   A: What do / are you mean / meaning? We have / 're having a lot of garlic.
            d.   **e.**   **f.**

   B: No, we don't / aren't. I used it all in the sauce!
              g.

2 **ACTION OR NON-ACTION •** *Complete the conversations with the correct form of the verbs in parentheses.*

1. **A:** Hi. What ____are____ you ____doing____?
   a. (do)

   B: I _____ a movie on TV.
   b. (watch)

   A: _____ it good?
   c. (be)

   B: I _____. It just started.
   d. (not know)

   A: It _____ interesting. What language _____ they _____?
   e. (look)   **f. (speak)**

   B: Italian. I _____ to understand it.
   g. (try)

2. **A:** Something _____ good.
   a. (smell)

   B: I _____ coffee. _____ you _____ some?
   b. (make)   **c. (want)**

   A: No, thanks. I _____ a glass of milk.
   d. (drink)

3. **A:** What _____ this word _____?
   a. (mean)

   B: I _____. _____ you _____ a dictionary?
   b. (not know)   **c. (have)**

   A: Yes. I _____ at it right now, but I _____ the definition.
   d. (look)   **e. (not understand)**

3 **ACTION OR NON-ACTION •** *Look at the picture. Complete the paragraph with the correct form of the verbs from the box.*

answer	~~be~~	be	be	hear	look
ring	see	think	want	watch	

Klaus ____is____ at home. His favorite
1.

TV program _____ on, but he _____ it.
2.   **3.** *(negative)*

He _____ for his glasses.
4.

He _____ they are in the living room.
5.

They _____ on his head, but he _____
6.   **7.** *(negative)*

them. The phone _____.
8.

Klaus _____ it, but he _____ it.
9.   **10.** *(negative)*

He really _____ to find his glasses!
11.

Present Progressive and Simple Present

1 **PRESENT PROGRESSIVE OR SIMPLE PRESENT: STATEMENTS** • *Complete the sentences with the correct form of the verbs in parentheses.*

1. Monique ___isn't reading___ the paper now.
    (not read)

2. She always _____ the news on TV.
    (watch)

3. Her brother usually _____ TV with her.
    (not watch)

4. Listen! The reporter _____ the race.
    (describe)

5. She _____ from Pamplona.
    (report)

6. She usually _____ in Spain.
    (not work)

7. She almost always _____ from Paris.
    (report)

8. Look! The race _____.
    (start)

9. They _____ in this race every year.
    (run)

10. Monique's friends never _____ the race.
    (watch)

11. They usually _____ it.
    (not enjoy)

12. The race _____ now.
    (end)

13. The runners _____ the finish line.
    (cross)

14. Monique _____ to watch more TV now.
    (not want)

15. She _____ the TV off.
    (turn)

2 **PRESENT PROGRESSIVE AND SIMPLE PRESENT** • *Complete the conversations with the correct form of the verbs in parentheses and short answers. Use contractions when possible.*

1. **A:** Hi! ___Are___ you ___studying___?
    a. (study)

    B: ___Yes, I am___. I have a test tomorrow.
    b.

2. **A:** Hi. What _____ you _____?
    a. (do)

    B: I _____ the paper.
    b. (read)

3. **A:** I _____ to leave now. What about you?
    a. (want)

    B: I _____ my homework. I _____ a few more minutes. OK?
    b. (do) **c. (need)**

4. **A:** When _____ your sister _____ to the gym?
   a. (go)

   B: Every morning. She always _____ a half an hour there before work.
   b. (spend)

5. **A:** _____ you _____ Sonia's number?
   a. (know)

   B: No. I _____ her e-mail address. _____ you _____ it?
   b. (have)   c. (want)

3 | **PRESENT PROGRESSIVE AND SIMPLE PRESENT: QUESTIONS AND SHORT ANSWERS** • *Da Ming is a reporter. Look at his morning schedule. Complete the questions with the correct form of the words in parentheses and write short answers.*

Morning Schedule	
7:00 A.M. get up	10:00 meet with Carlos
7:30 exercise	11:00 work on evening news
8:00 drive to work	12:00 lunch
9:00 report morning news	

1. **Q:** It's 7:00. _____Is he getting up now?_____
   (get up / now)

   A: _____Yes, he is._____

2. **Q:** _____
   (usually exercise / at 7:00)

   A: _____

3. **Q:** What time _____
   (usually / exercise)

   A: _____

4. **Q:** It's 8:00. _____
   (take the bus / now)

   A: _____

5. **Q:** What time _____
   (report / the morning news)

   A: _____

6. **Q:** It's 10:00. _____
   (meet with Carlos / now)

   A: _____

7. **Q:** _____
   (usually / report the news / at 11:00)

   A: _____

8. **Q:** It's noon. _____
   (eat lunch / now)

   A: _____

UNIT 9

The Imperative

1 **AFFIRMATIVE AND NEGATIVE** • *Complete with affirmative and negative imperative sentences.*

AFFIRMATIVE	**NEGATIVE**
1. Open your books.	*Don't open your books.*
2. *Look at the photo.*	Don't look at the photo.
3. Come here.	_____
4. Use a pen.	_____
5. _____	Don't turn right.
6. Close the window.	_____
7. Help your partner.	_____
8. _____	Don't come early.
9. Push the button.	_____
10. _____	Don't park here.
11. Use your dictionary.	_____
12. _____	Don't ask a classmate.

2 **AFFIRMATIVE AND NEGATIVE** • *Complete the teacher's instructions. Use contractions.*

TEACHER: Good morning, class. Please ____open____ your books to page 42 and
                                    1. (open)

_____ at the cartoon. _____ it now. Just _____ about it.
2. (look)   **3. (not read)**   **4. (think)**

Good. Now, _____ this question: Where are the people?
              5. (answer)

_____ the answer. _____ the class. Vanessa?
6. (not write)   **7. (tell)**

VANESSA: In a museum.

TEACHER: Right. Now _____ the cartoon and _____ the Check Point.
                      8. (read)   **9. (do)**

Please _____ a pen. _____ a pencil.
        10. (not use)   **11. (use)**

Now _____ your answer with a classmate.
      12. (check)

Do you have the same answer?

3 **AFFIRMATIVE AND NEGATIVE • Complete the sentences. Choose between affirmative and negative.**

1. The children are sleeping. Please _____ be _____ quiet.
   (be)
2. The oven is hot. _____ it.
   (touch)
3. The meeting is at 10:00. Please _____ on time.
   (come)
4. _____ nervous. Everything will be OK.
   (be)
5. _____ the instructions. They are very clear.
   (read)
6. This is difficult. Please _____ me.
   (help)
7. _____ the milk. It smells bad.
   (drink)
8. Please _____ after 11:00. I go to bed at 10:00.
   (call)
9. _____ the soup. It's very good.
   (taste)
10. _____ here. There's a NO PARKING sign.
    (park)
11. _____ your umbrella. It's going to rain.
    (take)
12. _____ the window. It's cold in here.
    (open)

4 **AFFIRMATIVE AND NEGATIVE • Look at the map. Complete the directions to the English Language Institute (ELI). Use the correct words from the box. Choose between affirmative and negative.**

| Be | Go | Make | make | Park | pass | S~~t~~art | Stay | Turn | turn | turn |

1. _____ Start _____ at Third and Pine.
2. _____ to Elm Street.
3. _____ left on Elm. _____ right.
   (Elm is a one-way street.)
4. _____ on Elm for two streets (until First).
5. _____ a right turn on First.
6. _____ a left turn.
   (First is also a one-way street.)
7. At Oak Street, _____ right.
8. _____ careful! _____
   Third Street. That's too far.
9. _____ in front of 23 Oak Street.
   That's the ELI building!

SelfTest

Circle the letter of the correct answer to complete each sentence.

> **EXAMPLE:** Carlos _____ a student.   **A B ⓒ D**
>   (A) are   (C) is
>   (B) does   (D) were

1. She _____ the bus.   **A B C D**
   (A) is liking   (C) likes
   (B) like   (D) is like

2. We always _____ TV in the evening.   **A B C D**
   (A) watch   (C) watches
   (B) watching   (D) doesn't watch

3. _____ you usually have coffee in the morning?   **A B C D**
   (A) Are   (C) Do
   (B) Am   (D) Does

4. _____ forget your books!   **A B C D**
   (A) Not   (C) No
   (B) You are   (D) Don't

5. Do you _____ a parking space?   **A B C D**
   (A) seeing   (C) sees
   (B) see   (D) 're seeing

6. These flowers _____ great.   **A B C D**
   (A) smelling   (C) are smelling
   (B) smells   (D) smell

7. I _____ cream and sugar in my coffee. **A B C D**
   (A) put never   (C) never put
   (B) 'm never put   (D) 's never put

8. _____ Aki study with you?   **A B C D**
   (A) Do   (C) Is
   (B) Does   (D) Are

9. _____ careful! The plate is hot.   **A B C D**
   (A) You   (C) Be
   (B) Are   (D) You are

10. Where _____ usually sit?   **A B C D**
    (A) do you   (C) you do
    (B) are you   (D) you are

11. Ari, _____ in.   **A B C D**
    (A) come please   (C) please you come
    (B) you come please   (D) please come

12. Why is he _____ ?   **A B C D**
    (A) smile   (C) smiling
    (B) smiles   (D) 's smiling

13. —Do you like your job?   **A B C D**
    —Yes, I _____ .
    (A) like   (C) am
    (B) do   (D) don't

14. The teacher sometimes _____ collect the homework.   **A B C D**
    (A) doesn't   (C) not
    (B) isn't   (D) don't

15. Celia _____ a lot of my friends.   **A B C D**
    (A) knows   (C) know
    (B) knowing   (D) 're knowing

SECTION TWO

Each sentence has four underlined parts. The four underlined parts are marked A, B, C, and D. Circle the letter of the part that is NOT CORRECT.

EXAMPLE:
Carla <u>is</u> a student, but she <u>are</u> <u>not</u> in school <u>today</u>.   A (B) C D
   A   B C   D

16. <u>Do</u> you <u>often</u> <u>going</u> to the museum on Saturday<u>?</u>   **A B C D**
   A   B   C   D

17. <u>Please</u> <u>you</u> <u>be</u> careful because the traffic <u>is</u> bad today.   **A B C D**
   A   B C   D

18. Those cookies <u>look</u> good, but <u>they</u> <u>doesn't</u> <u>taste</u> very good.   **A B C D**
              A   B   C   D

19. We <u>no</u> <u>want</u> to call Ana because she <u>isn't</u> <u>working</u> today.   **A B C D**
      A   B   C   D

20. Jana, <u>please</u> <u>comes</u> in and <u>close</u> the door<u>.</u>   **A B C D**
         A   B   C   D

21. She <u>don't</u> <u>feel</u> good right now, so <u>she's</u> <u>going</u> home.   **A B C D**
      A   B   C D

22. <u>Never he</u> <u>drinks</u> coffee at <u>night</u> because it <u>keeps</u> him awake.   **A B C D**
   A   B   C   D

23. <u>I'm not</u> <u>understand</u> Todd because he <u>always</u> <u>speaks</u> too fast.   **A B C D**
   A   B   C   D

24. We <u>always</u> <u>eat</u> dinner at seven, so <u>please</u> <u>no</u> be late.   **A B C D**
      A   B   C D

25. Li <u>often</u> <u>works</u> late, and she <u>works sometimes</u> <u>on Saturday</u>.   **A B C D**
   A   B   C   D

UNIT 10 — The Past of *Be*

1 AFFIRMATIVE STATEMENTS • *Complete the sentences with* **was** *or* **were**.

1. We _____were_____ at the museum yesterday.
2. Our teacher _____ there too.
3. The dinosaur exhibit _____ great.
4. Some dinosaurs _____ very, very big.
5. Lunch _____ good.
6. It _____ in the museum cafeteria.
7. My classmates _____ happy with the trip.
8. I _____ happy too.

2 NEGATIVE STATEMENTS • *Complete the sentences with* **wasn't** *or* **weren't**.

1. Sonia _____wasn't_____ in class yesterday.
2. She and her sister _____ at the museum.
3. Some dinosaurs _____ very big.
4. The museum _____ very expensive.
5. The dinosaur exhibit _____ too crowded.
6. My classmates and I _____ bored.
7. The cafeteria food _____ bad.
8. I _____ tired after the trip.

3 THERE WAS *OR* THERE WERE • *Complete the sentences with* **there was** *or* **there were**.

1. _____There were_____ a lot of people at the museum.
2. _____ a special exhibit about dinosaurs.
3. _____ many different kinds of dinosaurs.
4. _____ cheap tickets for students.
5. _____ a lot students in the cafeteria.
6. _____ a special lunch of soup and a sandwich.
7. _____ some very good desserts.
8. _____ a delicious chocolate cake.

24

4 **YES/NO QUESTIONS AND SHORT ANSWERS •** *Complete the questions and write short answers.*

1. **Q:** _____Were_____ you at school yesterday?

   A: ____Yes, I was____ . I'm always at school!

2. **Q:** _____ Jason there too?

   A: _____. Jason is in Australia with his family.

3. **Q:** _____ the homework easy?

   A: _____. It's never easy.

4. **Q:** _____ lunch good?

   A: _____. I love the pizza in the school cafeteria!

5. **Q:** _____ the students late to class this morning?

   A: _____. They're always early.

6. **Q:** _____ Mr. O'Neill early too?

   A: _____. His train was late.

7. **Q:** _____ the class interesting yesterday?

   A: _____. I always enjoy it.

5 **WH- QUESTIONS •** *Read the answers. Then ask questions about the underlined words.*

1. **Q:** Where were you? _____

   A: We were at a movie.

2. **Q:** _____

   A: Lia was with us.

3. **Q:** _____

   A: The movie was two hours long.

4. **Q:** _____

   A: It was over at 3:30.

5. **Q:** _____

   A: The movie was at the Cinema Five.

6. **Q:** _____

   A: The tickets were $5.

7. **Q:** _____

   A: It was about dinosaurs.

8. **Q:** _____

   A: It was very interesting.

UNIT 11

The Simple Past of Regular Verbs: Statements

1 **SPELLING** • *Add -d or -ed to these verbs. Make all necessary spelling changes.*

1. paint _painted_
2. work _____
3. like _____
4. study _____
5. smell _____
6. hug _____
7. want _____
8. hate _____

9. marry _____
10. help _____
11. stop _____
12. try _____
13. live _____
14. arrive _____
15. hurry _____
16. play _____

2 **AFFIRMATIVE STATEMENTS** • *Complete the sentences with the simple past form of the verbs in parentheses.*

1. Frida Kahlo was born in 1907. She _____ _lived_ _____
   (live)
   in Mexico City.

2. At first, Frida Kahlo _____ to be a doctor.
   (want)

3. After a serious accident, she _____ her plans.
   (change)

4. She _____ painting from her bed.
   (start)

5. She _____ pictures of her family and friends.
   (paint)

6. She never _____ art in school.
   (study)

7. One day, she _____ her paintings to the famous
   (show)
   Mexican painter Diego Rivera.

8. He _____ her work. He also _____ Kahlo.
   (love)   (love)

9. The two painters _____ in 1929.
   (marry)

10. They _____ later, but they _____ again and
    (separate)   (marry)
    _____ together.
    (stay)

11. Kahlo _____ in 1954. Today, she and her work are very famous.
    (die)

3 **NEGATIVE STATEMENTS** • *Talia and Antonio were very different as students. Read about Talia.*
Write negative sentences about Antonio.

1. Talia loved art. Antonio *didn't love art.*
2. She studied very hard. He _____
3. She hurried to school every day. He _____
4. She always arrived early. He _____
5. She started at 8:00. He _____
6. She painted beautiful pictures. He _____
7. She worked a lot. He _____
8. She liked painting. He _____
9. She used bright colors. He _____
10. She tried new things. He _____
11. She worried about her grades. He _____
12. She worked late every day. He _____

4 **AFFIRMATIVE AND NEGATIVE STATEMENTS** • *Correct these sentences about famous painters.*
Use the information in the chart.

ARTIST'S NAME	YEARS	PLACE OF BIRTH	EDUCATION	FAMOUS PAINTING
Edvard Munch	1863–1944	Norway	Norway and France	*The Scream*
Vincent Van Gogh	1853–1890	the Netherlands	Belgium and France	*Starry Night*
Georgia O'Keeffe	1887–1986	United States	United States	*City Night*

1. Edvard Munch lived in Sweden. *He didn't live in Sweden. He lived in Norway.*
2. He studied in England. _____
3. He painted *City Night*. _____
4. He died in 1863. _____
5. Vincent Van Gogh painted *The Scream*. _____
6. He lived in Norway. _____
7. He moved to Italy and Spain. _____
8. He died at the age of 67. _____
9. Georgia O'Keeffe lived in Canada. _____
10. She studied in France. _____
11. She painted *Starry Night*. _____
12. She lived a short life. _____

The Simple Past of Irregular Verbs: Statements

1 **FORM • Complete with the correct form of the verbs.**

	PRESENT	PAST		PRESENT	PAST
1.	think	_thought_	10.	get	_____
2.	_____	left	11.	do	_____
3.	go	_____	12.	_____	met
4.	am	_____	13.	see	_____
5.	_____	came	14.	_____	felt
6.	begin	_____	15.	hear	_____
7.	is	_____	16.	find	_____
8.	has	_____	17.	_____	lost
9.	_____	bought	18.	teach	_____

2 **AFFIRMATIVE STATEMENTS • Read about today. Write sentences about yesterday.**

1. The boat is leaving now. What about the train?

   The train left yesterday.

2. Carlos is going to the movies. What about Enrique?

   _____

3. The Thompsons are here. What about the Botteros?

   _____

4. Class 101 is having a test. What about Class 202?

   _____

5. Sonia is getting a new computer. What about Chen-Lu?

   _____

6. Dan is making dinner. What about Tomás?

   _____

7. Lisa is doing the homework. What about Jason?

   _____

8. I'm reading the newspaper. What about Mr. Thompson?

   _____

3 **NEGATIVE STATEMENTS** • *Write negative sentences.*

1. We went by ship. Wolfgang _____ *didn't go by ship.* _____

2. Anton left yesterday. Mona _____

3. I knew the captain. They _____

4. She saw a movie. I _____

5. They slept in a hotel. We _____

6. We were in Spain. Our friend _____

7. We took the train. She _____

8. They spent a lot of money. We _____

9. We met interesting people. They _____

10. We had a good time. They _____

4 **AFFIRMATIVE AND NEGATIVE STATEMENTS** • *Look at the information in the ad. Complete the sentences with the correct form of the verbs in parentheses.*

ADVENTURE TRIP—*South America and Antarctica*

Round trip from: Ushuaia, Argentina
Date: January 15, 2003
Ship: the *Hanseatic*
Passengers: 184
Days: 10
Sights: icebergs, water birds, sea animals
Price: from $6,795 per person
   (includes all meals in ship's dining room)

1. The trip _____ *didn't begin* _____ in England. It _____ in Argentina.
   (begin)   (begin)

2. The ship _____ in April. It _____ on January 15.
   (leave)   (leave)

3. The round-trip adventure _____ a week. It _____ ten days.
                             (take)   (take)

4. The boat _____ 1,000 passengers. It _____ only 184.
            (have)   (have)

5. It _____ very expensive. It _____ almost $7,000 per person.
      (be)   (cost)

6. The ship _____ to Antarctica. It _____ to the Arctic.
            (go)   (go)

7. Passengers _____ icebergs and sea animals. They _____ trees
              (see)   (see)
   and flowers.

8. Passengers _____ on the ship. They _____ in restaurants.
              (eat)   (eat)

UNIT 13 The Simple Past:
Questions

1 **YES/NO QUESTIONS** • *Read about Elissa. Ask questions about Todd.*

1. She went to Egypt. _____ Did he go to Egypt too? _____

2. She flew there on Monday. _____

3. She stayed at a hotel. _____

4. She ate dinner there. _____

5. She went on a tour. _____

6. She saw the Pyramids. _____

7. She met a lot of interesting people. _____

8. She sent Kishana a postcard. _____

9. She had a great time. _____

10. She came home yesterday. _____

2 **SHORT ANSWERS** • *Answer these questions.*

1. **A:** Did you enjoy your trip?

   B: _____ Yes, I did _____ . I had a great time.

2. **A:** Did you like the food?

   B: _____ . It was really good.

3. **A:** Did you visit your old professor?

   B: _____ . He wasn't there.

4. **A:** Did your children go with you?

   B: _____ . My son and my daughter went with me.

5. **A:** Did your son have a good time?

   B: _____ . He was sick the whole time.

6. **A:** That's too bad. What about your daughter? Did she enjoy the trip?

   B: _____ . She loved it.

7. **A:** Did you and your children see a lot of the country?

   B: _____ . We rented a car and drove around a lot.

8. **A:** Did you meet many people?

   B: _____ . We met a lot of interesting people.

3 **WH-QUESTIONS** • *Read the answers. Then ask questions about the underlined words.*

1. **Q:** _How many books did you read?_
   A: I read <u>five</u> books about Spain.

2. **Q:** _____
   A: They flew <u>to Barcelona</u>.

3. **Q:** _____
   A: They went there <u>because they love it</u>.

4. **Q:** _____
   A: They left <u>at 11:30</u>.

5. **Q:** _____
   A: She stayed <u>at a hotel</u>.

6. **Q:** _____
   A: The trip cost <u>$800</u>.

7. **Q:** _____
   A: He visited <u>his teacher</u>.

8. **Q:** _____
   A: They ate <u>fish</u> every day.

9. **Q:** _____
   A: They were there <u>in the summer</u>.

10. **Q:** _____
    A: They wore <u>light clothes</u>.

4 **YES/NO QUESTIONS, WH- QUESTIONS, SHORT ANSWERS** • *Look at the picture. Complete the questions with the correct form of the verbs in parentheses and write short answers.*

1. **Q:** Where ____did____ they ____go____?
   (go)
   A: ____Mexico City____.

2. **Q:** _____ they _____ the train?
   (take)
   A: _____.

3. **Q:** How _____ they _____?
   (travel)
   A: _____.

4. **Q:** What time _____ the plane _____?
   (leave)
   A: _____.

5. **Q:** _____ they _____ yesterday?
   (leave)
   A: _____.

6. **Q:** _____ their daughter _____ too?
   (go)
   A: _____.

7. **Q:** How many pieces of luggage _____ the man _____?
   (have)
   A: _____.

8. **Q:** _____ the woman _____ two pieces too?
   (have)
   A: _____.

9. **Q:** _____ the man _____ his camera?
   (take)
   A: _____.

10. **Q:** _____ they _____ happy?
    (seem)
    A: _____.

Yesterday

SelfTest

SECTION ONE

Circle the letter of the correct answer to complete each sentence.

EXAMPLE: Carlos _____ a student.	A B Ⓒ D
(A) are (C) is	
(B) does (D) were	

1. Did you _____ to school yesterday?   **A B C D**
   (A) went   (C) go
   (B) goes   (D) going

2. Where _____ you last week?   **A B C D**
   (A) were   (C) are
   (B) was   (D) is

3. I _____ in school.   **A B C D**
   (A) was no   (C) were
   (B) wasn't   (D) aren't

4. When _____ call the doctor?   **A B C D**
   (A) she did   (C) did she
   (B) she was   (D) was she

5. She didn't _____ her last night.   **A B C D**
   (A) called   (C) calls
   (B) call   (D) calling

6. Why _____ so unhappy yesterday?   **A B C D**
   (A) you were   (C) are you
   (B) you are   (D) were you

7. There _____ a lot of problems at work.   **A B C D**
   (A) were   (C) had
   (B) was   (D) have

8. —Did you meet Sonia last week?   **A B C D**
   —No, I _____. I met her last year.
   (A) don't   (C) didn't
   (B) not   (D) wasn't

9. — Were you and Sonia in school together?   **A B C D**
   — Yes, _____.
   (A) I was   (C) we are
   (B) we were   (D) she was

10. She studied art _____.   **A B C D**
    (A) now   (C) tomorrow
    (B) rarely   (D) last year

11. Her family _____ in Quebec in 2003.　　　　A B C D
    (A) lives　　　　　　(C) live
    (B) lived　　　　　　(D) are living

12. _____ you study French there?　　　　A B C D
    (A) Does　　　　　　(C) Did
    (B) Were　　　　　　(D) Are

13. He didn't _____ the party at 11:00.　　　　A B C D
    (A) left　　　　　　(C) leaves
    (B) leave　　　　　　(D) leaving

14. —Did you stay with your sister last night?　　　　A B C D
    —Yes, _____.
    (A) I did　　　　　　(C) I stayed with
    (B) did I　　　　　　(D) do

15. _____ there a lot of people there?　　　　A B C D
    (A) Were　　　　　　(C) Did
    (B) Was　　　　　　(D) Have

SECTION TWO

Each sentence has four underlined parts. The four underlined parts of the sentence are marked A, B, C, and D. Circle the letter of the part that is NOT CORRECT.

EXAMPLE:

Carla <u>is</u> a student, but she <u>are</u> <u>not</u> in school <u>today</u>.　　　　A (B) C D
　　　A　　　　　　　　B　C　　　　　　D

16. We <u>took</u> a trip to Spain <u>last month</u>, but we <u>didn't</u> <u>flew</u> there.　　　　A B C D
　　　　A　　　　　　　　B　　　　　　C　　D

17. I <u>didn't</u> <u>swim</u>, but I <u>sailed</u> a boat and <u>walk</u> on the beach.　　　　A B C D
　　　A　　B　　　　　C　　　　　　D

18. <u>Did</u> you <u>haved</u> a good time at the party <u>last night</u> <u>?</u>　　　　A B C D
　　A　　　B　　　　　　　　　　C　　D

19. Nadia <u>didn't</u> <u>went</u> to school <u>yesterday</u> because she <u>was</u> sick.　　　　A B C D
　　　　A　　B　　　　　C　　　　　　D

20. <u>Why</u> <u>Tom did</u> <u>call</u> last week?　　　　A B C D
　　A　　B　　C　　D

21. <u>Where</u> <u>did</u> he <u>study</u> after school<u>.</u>　　　　A B C D
　　A　　B　　C　　　　D

22. The movie <u>ended</u> late, so <u>we</u> <u>don't</u> <u>go</u> for coffee last night.　　　　A B C D
　　　　A　　　　　B　　C　D

23. The store <u>were</u> <u>not</u> crowded, so I <u>stayed</u> and <u>bought</u> food.　　　　A B C D
　　　　A　　B　　　　　　C　　　D

24. <u>Why</u> <u>she was</u> afraid when <u>she</u> <u>saw</u> that dog?　　　　A B C D
　　A　　B　　　　　C　　D

25. <u>Did</u> <u>he</u> <u>takes</u> a lot of photos on his vacation<u>?</u>　　　　A B C D
　　A　　B　　C　　　　　　　　D

UNIT 14

The Future with *Be going to*

1 **CONTRACTIONS** • *Rewrite these sentences. Use contractions.*

1. I am going to leave now.   I'm going to leave now.

2. We are not going to hurry.   _____ OR _____

3. It is going to rain.   _____

4. You are going to be late.   _____

5. She is not going to like it.   _____ OR _____

6. He is going to call you.   _____

7. They are going to fly.   _____

8. I am not going to stay.   _____

9. We are going to study.   _____

10. It is not going to be hard.   _____ OR _____

2 **AFFFIRMATIVE AND NEGATIVE STATEMENTS** • *Complete the sentences with the correct form of the verbs in parentheses. Use contractions when possible.*

1. ___I'm not going to have___ lunch. I'm not hungry.
   (have)

2. We _____ to the supermarket. We need fruit and vegetables.
   (go)

3. He _____ a new computer. His old one is fine.
   (buy)

4. I'm studying. The teacher _____ us a test tomorrow.
   (give)

5. Take your umbrella. It _____.
   (rain)

6. You don't need a jacket. It _____ cold.
   (be)

7. She _____ a vacation. She doesn't have time.
   (take)

8. They _____ late. There's a lot of traffic.
   (be)

9. I _____ the train. I bought a ticket yesterday.
   (take)

10. Hurry. The movie _____ in a few minutes.
    (start)

11. The train _____ on time. It's having engine problems.
    (arrive)

12. My friends _____ me at the station. They are there now.
    (meet)

3 **YES/NO QUESTIONS AND SHORT ANSWERS** • *Complete the questions with the correct form of the verbs in parentheses and write short answers.*

1. **Q:** _____Are_____ you _____going to call_____ Boris?
   (call)
   A: _No, I'm not_. I lost his number.

2. **Q:** _____ it _____?
   (rain)
   A: _____. There's not a cloud in the sky.

3. **Q:** _____ he _____ dinner?
   (make)
   A: _____. He's cutting the vegetables now.

4. **Q:** _____ we _____ late?
   (be)
   A: _____. Don't worry. It's still early.

5. **Q:** _____ I _____ a jacket?
   (need)
   A: _____. It's cool in the meeting room.

6. **Q:** _____ you _____ for a new job?
   (look)
   A: _____. I like my job.

4 **WH- QUESTIONS** • *Read the answers and then ask questions about the underlined words.*

1. **Q:** The conference is tomorrow. _____When is it going to start?_____
   A: It's going to start <u>at 10:00</u>.

2. **Q:** _____
   A: <u>A hundred</u> people are going to be there.

3. **Q:** _____
   A: It's going to be <u>at a big hotel</u>.

4. **Q:** _____
   A: She's going to buy <u>a ticket</u>.

5. **Q:** _____
   A: It's going to cost <u>ten euros</u>.

6. **Q:** _____
   A: <u>Professor Chang</u> is going to speak.

7. **Q:** _____
   A: It's going to end <u>at noon</u>.

8. **Q:** _____
   A: He's going to leave early <u>because he has a meeting</u>.

The Future with *Will*

1   **CONTRACTIONS** • *Rewrite these sentences. Use contractions.*

1. I will see you tomorrow. <u>I'll see you tomorrow.</u>

2. It will be nice. _____

3. It will not rain. _____

4. They will come with us. _____

5. He will not be late. _____

6. She will drive him here. _____

7. You will like them. _____

8. We will have a good time. _____

2   **AFFIRMATIVE AND NEGATIVE STATEMENTS** • *Complete the sentences with the correct form of the verbs in parentheses.*

1. Guido <u> won't be </u> at work tomorrow.
   (not be)

2. He _____ at home.
   (be)

3. You look tired. I _____ you.
   (help)

4. I'm sorry, but I _____ that question.
   (not answer)

5. Sara has Tony's phone number, but she _____ it to me.
   (not give)

6. They _____ to come on time.
   (try)

7. Our vacation _____ cheap.
   (not be)

8. It _____ fun.
   (be)

9. We _____ you there.
   (see)

10. My sister _____ you at the hotel.
    (call)

11. I _____ to her before Tuesday.
    (not speak)

12. My sister's boss _____ her a promotion.
    (not give)

13. She _____ for more money.
    (ask)

14. She _____ her job.
    (not quit)

3 **YES/NO QUESTIONS AND SHORT ANSWERS** • *Complete the conversations with the correct form of the verbs in parentheses.*

1. **A:** _____Will_____ you _____be_____ home tomorrow afternoon?
   (be)

   B: _No, I won't_ . I have school every afternoon.

2. **A:** _____ you _____ Raoul tomorrow?
   (see)

   B: _____ . He's not in town.

3. **A:** _____ Marta _____ happy with her new job?
   (be)

   B: _____ . It's interesting and the people are very nice.

4. **A:** _____ Mehmet _____ to the meeting?
   (come)

   B: _____ . He has another meeting at the same time.

5. **A:** _____ the train _____ crowded?
   (be)

   B: _____ . Most people don't travel at this time.

6. **A:** _____ the children _____ the movie?
   (like)

   B: _____ . It's a great movie for kids.

7. **A:** _____ it _____ cold in the park?
   (get)

   B: _____ . Take a sweater.

4 **WH- QUESTIONS AND ANSWERS** • *Unscramble the words to ask questions. Choose the correct answers from the box.*

At 8:00	~~At my party~~	At the supermarket	By train
Fifteen	My classmates	Jeans	Twenty bottles

1. **A:** _Where will you be Friday night?_ **B:** _At my party._
   (you / Friday night / where / will / be)

2. **A:** _____ **B:** _____
   (invite / you / who / will)

3. **A:** _____ **B:** _____
   (will / people / how many / come)

4. **A:** _____ **B:** _____
   (the guests / when / will / arrive)

5. **A:** _____ **B:** _____
   (you / will / wear / what)

6. **A:** _____ **B:** _____
   (Enrique / how / will / to the party / get)

7. **A:** _____ **B:** _____
   (you / soda / will / buy / how much)

8. **A:** _____ **B:** _____
   (it / will / you / where / buy)

SelfTest IV

Circle the letter of the correct answer to complete each sentence.

> **EXAMPLE:** Carlos _____ a student.   A B Ⓒ D
> (A) are   (C) is
> (B) does   (D) were

1. _____ they going to be home late?   A B C D
   (A) Are   (C) Will
   (B) Is   (D) Do

2. I'll _____ that bag for you.   A B C D
   (A) carry   (C) will carry
   (B) to carry   (D) carrying

3. Why _____ going to buy a new computer?   A B C D
   (A) they are   (C) do they
   (B) they   (D) are they

4. —Is it going to rain today?   A B C D
   —Yes, _____.
   (A) it's   (C) it's going
   (B) it is   (D) it rains

5. I _____ be home before six o'clock.   A B C D
   (A) not   (C) will no
   (B) no will   (D) won't

6. Darryl is going _____ to the meeting.   A B C D
   (A) drive   (C) drives
   (B) to drive   (D) driving

7. I _____ meet you after lunch.   A B C D
   (A) going to   (C) 'll
   (B) 'm going   (D) 's going to

8. Where _____ be at noon?   A B C D
   (A) are you going   (C) are you going to
   (B) you are going   (D) you are going to

9. Look at that guy up there! He _____!   A B C D
   (A) 's going to fall (C) falling
   (B) will fall   (D) falls

10. —Will you see Antoine at the meeting tomorrow?   A B C D
    —Yes, I _____.
    (A) do   (C) will
    (B) am   (D) speak

11. He _____ be at school.   A B C D
    (A) no will   (C) won't
    (B) doesn't   (D) will no

12. I _____ you at 5:00.   A B C D
    (A) meet   (C) 'll meet
    (B) meeting   (D) going to meet

SECTION TWO

Each sentence has four underlined parts. The four underlined parts are marked
A, B, C, and D. Circle the letter of the part that is NOT CORRECT.

EXAMPLE:

Carla is a student, but she are not in school today.   A Ⓑ C D
     A   B C   D

13. I'm not going have lunch here because I'm going to leave early.   A B C D
      A   B   C   D

14. Why he is going to drive to work?   A B C D
       A B   C   D

15. Are you going to be home last night?   A B C D
        A   B C   D

16. Will Teri picks up pizza on the way home, or will we eat out?   A B C D
           A   B C D

17. Why they are going to go to work tomorrow?   A B C D
     A   B   C   D

18. Where he going to stay on his trip to London?   A B C D
       A   B   C   D

19. Are going to your friends come for dinner tomorrow night?   A B C D
     A   B   C   D

20. I no will be late because Jon's going to give me a ride at 7:00. A B C D
      A   B   C   D

21. What are you going do after class?   A B C D
     A   B   C D

22. Will we going to see you soon?   A B C D
       A   B   C D

23. I'm going to have the fish, and my friend will has the chicken. A B C D
       A   B   C D

24. Will you going to go to the movies with us tonight?   A B C D
     A   B   C   D

25. Where will we be at this time next year.   A B C D
        A B C   D

Word Order: Statements

1 **STATEMENTS WITH ONE OBJECT OR TWO OBJECTS •** *Read these sentences. Check the correct column.*

	ONE OBJECT	TWO OBJECTS
1. My mother bought me the book.		✔
2. I read it at night.		
3. I gave a copy to my friend.		
4. She liked it a lot.		
5. She showed it to her friends.		
6. Her friends told their friends the story.		
7. They lent the book to other friends.		
8. They saw the movie too.		

2 **STATEMENTS WITH ONE OBJECT •** *Put the words in the correct order.*

1. Sally • a letter • wrote

Sally wrote a letter.

2. a stamp • bought • at the post office • she

_____

3. mailed • yesterday • she • the letter

_____

4. received • her friend • on • Tuesday • it

_____

5. it • read • at school • she

_____

6. understand • didn't • the letter • she

_____

7. she • her friend • call • didn't

_____

8. e-mailed • her friend • she • the next day

_____

40

3 **STATEMENTS WITH TWO OBJECTS** • *Complete the sentences. Choose the correct object from each column.*

DIRECT OBJECTS	INDIRECT OBJECTS
a cake	you
chocolate	~~her~~
my notes	us
~~all the books~~	me
a map	them
her new CD	him

1. John's daughter loves Harry Potter. He bought ___her all the books.___
2. My brother loves desserts. I baked _____
3. I love music. Pat showed _____ to _____
4. My cousins are going to visit me for the first time.
   I e-mailed _____ to _____
5. We love candy. Our friends brought _____
6. You weren't in class yesterday. I'll show _____

4 **STATEMENTS WITH TWO OBJECTS** • *Rewrite these sentences.*

1. He sent the letter to his brother.
   He sent his brother the letter.

2. She gave her sister the present.
   She gave the present to her sister.

3. I read the story to my little brother.
   _____

4. They sold the house to Mr. and Mrs. Hampton.
   _____

5. She showed me her new jacket.
   _____

6. I handed my report to the teacher.
   _____

7. He sold Jason his bike.
   _____

8. Jason told him a story.
   _____

Word Order:
Wh- Questions

1   **QUESTIONS ABOUT THE OBJECT OR TIME AND PLACE •** *Ask questions about the underlined words.*

1. He watches TV <u>in the living room</u>.
   Where does he watch TV?

2. His favorite show begins <u>at 7:00 P.M.</u>
   _____

3. He watches it <u>because it's interesting</u>.
   _____

4. He likes <u>the host of the show</u>.
   _____

5. Last night he answered <u>ten</u> questions.
   _____

6. He always eats <u>dessert</u> during the show.
   _____

7. The show ends <u>at 7:30</u>.
   _____

8. He calls <u>his girlfriend</u> after the show.
   _____

2   **QUESTIONS ABOUT THE SUBJECT •** *Ask questions about the underlined words.*

1. <u>Malov and Natasha</u> watched the show.
   Who watched the show?

2. <u>Four million</u> people saw it.
   _____

3. <u>Natasha</u> liked it.
   _____

4. <u>She</u> knew a lot of the answers.
   _____

5. <u>Something unusual</u> happened.
   _____

42

6. <u>A teenager</u> won a lot of money.

_____

7. <u>He</u> gave the money to a hospital.

_____

8. <u>A hundred</u> people called the show.

_____

3 **QUESTIONS ABOUT THE SUBJECT, OBJECT, OR TIME AND PLACE** • *Natasha wrote a letter, but you can't read some parts of it. Ask questions about those parts.*

Hi.

I saw _____ last night. We watched _____. After the program we went to _____. _____ went with us. I had a really nice time. We ate _____ whole pizzas. It was great, but it cost _____! We went home at _____ because _____.

I had a really nice time.

☺ Natasha

1. Who did you see last night? **5.** _____

2. _____ **6.** _____

3. _____ **7.** _____

4. _____ **8.** _____

4 **ANSWERS** • *Now answer the questions in Exercise 3. Use the words from the box.*

Three	10:00 P.M.	To an Italian restaurant	Malov's sister
$40	~~Malov~~	Malov felt sick	A game show

1. Malov. **5.** _____

2. _____ **6.** _____

3. _____ **7.** _____

4. _____ **8.** _____

SelfTest V

Circle the letter of the correct answer to complete each sentence.

EXAMPLE: Carlos _____ a student.   A   B   Ⓒ   D

    (A) are   (C) is
    (B) does   (D) were

1. I mailed a book _____ my friend.   A   B   C   D
    (A) on   (C) is
    (B) to   (D) —

2. We _____.   A   B   C   D
    (A) watch TV at night   (C) at night TV watch
    (B) TV watch at night   (D) watch at night TV

3. When _____ going to move?   A   B   C   D
    (A) she is   (C) does she
    (B) she   (D) is she

4. Where _____ eat last night?   A   B   C   D
    (A) you did   (C) you
    (B) did you   (D) are you

5. She _____.   A   B   C   D
    (A) buys books here   (C) buys here books
    (B) here buys books   (D) books here buys

6. What _____?   A   B   C   D
    (A) in class happened   (C) happened in class
    (B) did happen in class   (D) did in class happen

7. —Who told you about the test?   A   B   C   D
    —_____.
    (A) Carla told me   (C) Yesterday
    (B) In class   (D) I told Carla

8. I showed _____ today.   A   B   C   D
    (A) it to him   (C) to him it
    (B) it him   (D) to it him

9. —_____ did you go?   A   B   C   D
    —At four o'clock.
    (A) When   (C) How
    (B) Where   (D) Why

10. Which shoes _____?   A   B   C   D
    (A) you bought   (C) did you buy
    (B) bought you   (D) you did buy

11. —Who _____ at the movies?
    —Marla saw them.
    (A) saw them   (C) did they see
    (B) they saw   (D) they did see

    A B C D

12. She showed _____ the test.
    (A) us   (C) we
    (B) to us   (D) to we

    A B C D

SECTION TWO

*Each sentence has four underlined parts. The four underlined parts are marked
A, B, C, and D. Circle the letter of the part that is NOT CORRECT.*

EXAMPLE:

Carla <u>is</u> a student, but she <u>are</u> <u>not</u> in school <u>today</u>.
   A   B   C   D

A (B) C D

13. <u>What</u> <u>you did</u> <u>tell</u> Alicia <u>last week</u>?
   A   B   C   D

    A B C D

14. <u>They</u> <u>gave</u> <u>to the teacher a book</u> on her <u>birthday</u>.
   A   B   C   D

    A B C D

15. <u>Where</u> <u>you mailed</u> <u>the letter</u> <u>yesterday</u>?
   A   B   C   D

    A B C D

16. He <u>the movie saw</u> <u>downtown</u> <u>last night</u>, and he <u>liked it</u>.
        A   B   C   D

    A B C D

17. <u>How many</u> <u>people</u> <u>did see</u> <u>the accident</u>?
   A   B   C   D

    A B C D

18. I <u>sent</u> an e-mail <u>you</u>, but you <u>didn't answer</u> <u>it</u>.
   A   B   C   D

    A B C D

19. <u>We</u> often <u>to the beach go</u> <u>in May</u>, but this year <u>we stayed</u> home.
   A   B   C   D

    A B C D

20. <u>Who</u> <u>you saw</u> <u>at the party</u> <u>last night</u>?
   A   B   C   D

    A B C D

21. <u>Why</u> <u>did you</u> show Tina <u>my letter</u> <u>.</u>
   A   B   C   D

    A B C D

22. <u>Which</u> book <u>you read</u> <u>in class</u> <u>last month</u>?
   A   B   C   D

    A B C D

23. <u>When</u> <u>they did</u> <u>tell</u> you about the <u>homework</u>?
   A   B   C   D

    A B C D

24. <u>What</u> <u>did</u> happened <u>in the library</u> <u>yesterday</u>?
   A   B   C   D

    A B C D

25. <u>Who</u> <u>gave</u> <u>you</u> <u>in the store</u> help?
   A   B   C   D

    A B C D

UNIT 18

Nouns: Common/Proper, Singular/Plural

1 **COMMON AND PROPER NOUNS** • *Match the common and proper nouns.*

COMMON NOUNS

_____h_____ **1.** country

_____ **2.** city

_____ **3.** language

_____ **4.** nationality

_____ **5.** business

_____ **6.** name of a person

_____ **7.** day

_____ **8.** month

PROPER NOUNS

a. Arabic

b. February

c. Mehmet

d. Mexican

e. Rome

f. Wednesday

g. Honda

h. Brazil

2 **PROPER NOUNS: CAPITALIZATION** • *Read these sentences. Capitalize the proper nouns.*

1. I will be at my brother's house in Seoul on sunday, november 9th.

2. My friend carmen is studying french in paris.

3. Dave works for sony records as an accountant.

4. Jorge is a chef at a mexican restaurant in texas.

5. Lola lives at 2342 main street in london.

3 **SINGULAR AND PLURAL NOUNS: SPELLING** • *Complete with the correct form of the noun. Write **X** if there is no singular form.*

SINGULAR NOUNS	PLURAL NOUNS	SINGULAR NOUNS	PLURAL NOUNS
1. store	stores	**8.** knife	_____
2. X	pants	**9.** box	_____
3. country	_____	**10.** _____	feet
4. man	_____	**11.** _____	people
5. _____	jeans	**12.** _____	scissors
6. child	_____	**13.** book	_____
7. _____	women	**14.** house	_____

4 **SINGULAR OR PLURAL** • *Read these sentences. Complete them with the correct form of the nouns and the verbs in parentheses.*

1. _____Stores_____ _____are_____ often crowded.
   (Store)   (be)

2. Many _____ _____ to shop online.
        (person)   (prefer)

3. An online _____ _____ convenient.
              (catalog)   (be)

4. An online _____ _____ always "open."
              (store)   (be)

5. An online _____ _____ the chance to shop twenty-four hours a day.
              (customer)   (have)

6. There _____ many online _____.
          (be)   (store)

7. Macy's department _____ _____ an online catalog.
                      (store)   (have)

8. Their online _____ _____ things from all over the world.
                 (store)   (sell)

9. Their _____ _____ nice.
          (shoe)   (look)

10. More _____ _____ online than _____.
          (woman)   (shop)   (man)

11. This week _____ _____ on sale.
              (earring)   (be)

12. Two _____ of _____ _____ never enough for me!
         (pair)   (earring)   (be)

5 **EDIT** • *Read this article. Find and correct nineteen mistakes in the use of nouns and the verbs and pronouns that go with them. The first mistake is already corrected.*

No Lines Online!

    I hate to shop for clothes. I don't like crowded ~~Stores~~ *stores*. In large stores, saleswoman and salesmen is too busy. In small stores, salespeoples are "too helpful": They don't leave you alone. In *all* store, the dressing rooms is uncomfortable.

    Clothes is important, but I don't buy it in stores because Time is important too. I shop online. There is many good things about online stores. First of all, they are always open: twenty-four hour a day, seven day a week. You can shop on a sunday or on a holiday. It's an easy and fast ways to shop. I finish my order with just a few click of my computer mouse, and my order arrives in just a few day. Best of all, it's comfortable. I can try on that new pair of jean in my own home.

    So, do you really hate to shop too? Stay home! No more standing on those long line! Shop online! Your order is just one clicks away!

UNIT 19 — Nouns: Count/Non-Count

1   **COUNT AND NON-COUNT NOUNS** • *Put these words in the correct column.*

apple	teacher	Spanish	salt
pen	spoon	number	soup
book	milk	health	homework

COUNT NOUNS

apple
_____
_____
_____
_____

NON-COUNT NOUNS

_____
_____
_____
_____

2   **SINGULAR OR PLURAL** • *Complete the sentences. Use the correct form of the nouns from Exercise 1.*

1. Rachel eats two ___apples___ every day.
2. Do you drink _____?
3. My brother read thirty _____ last summer.
4. Did the teacher give us math _____ yesterday?
5. Be careful! The _____ is very hot.
6. Anton doesn't smoke because he's worried about his _____.
7. This doesn't taste very good. It needs more _____.
8. Do you have a _____? I want to write a note.
9. Todd remembers all of his friends' phone _____.
10. Who are the best _____ at your school?
11. Do you speak _____?
12. How many _____ do we need on the dinner table?

3 **MEASURE WORDS** • *Write a shopping list with the words from the boxes. Choose one word from each box. Choose between singular and plural.*

can	~~bag~~	bottle		bread	~~chip~~	soup
bar	loaf	pound		soap	potato	water

1. _____1 bag of chips_____
2. _____
3. _____
4. _____
5. _____
6. _____

1. CHIPS 2. SOAP SOAP SOAP SOAP 3. SOUP SOUP

4. (bread loaf) 5. POTATOES 2 LBS 6. (bottles)

4 **VERBS WITH COUNT AND NON-COUNT NOUNS** • *Complete the conversation with the correct form of the words in parentheses.*

A: This _____tea_____ _____tastes_____ delicious.
  1. (tea)   2. (taste)

B: Would you like _____ in it?
           3. (milk)

A: No, thanks. I drank four _____ of _____ today. I think
                  4. (glass)   5. (milk)
  that's enough!

B: OK. What about _____? I baked them this morning.
           6. (cookie)

A: Sure. Mmmm. The _____ _____ great.
              7. (cookie)   8. (be)

B: Thanks. The _____ _____ easy. I'll give it to you.
           9. (recipe)   10. (be)

A: The chocolate _____ good, and the _____ _____
              11. (taste)   12. (nut)   13. (be)
  really good too.

B: The _____ _____ from France. I toast the _____
      14. (chocolate) 15. (come)   16. (nut)
  in the _____ before I add them.
         17. (oven)

A: What kind of _____ do you use?
              18. (sugar)

B: Brown. And lot of _____ _____ in the recipe too.
                 19. (butter)   20. (go)

A: What about _____? How many do you use?
           21. (egg)

B: Four.

Articles: *A/An* and *The*

1 **A OR AN** • *Write* **a** *or* **an**.

1. __a__ house
2. _____ old house
3. _____ apartment
4. _____ orange couch
5. _____ blue chair
6. _____ English class
7. _____ school
8. _____ university

9. _____ hospital
10. _____ mistake
11. _____ honest mistake
12. _____ minute
13. _____ hour
14. _____ umbrella
15. _____ ice cream cone
16. _____ chocolate ice cream cone

2 **A, AN, OR THE** • *Circle the correct words to complete the sentences.*

1. My friends are looking for (a)/ the new house.
2. A / An agent is helping them.
3. A / The agent shows them a lot of houses every week.
4. Last week, they saw a / the very nice house.
5. They both liked a / the house a lot.
6. It has two bedrooms and a / the large office.
7. They need a / an office because Isabel works at home.
8. She's a / the writer. She writes articles for a / the magazine.
9. Hugo is a / the cook.
10. He works in a / the center of town.
11. A / The restaurant has four other cooks.
12. Hugo wants to have a / the good kitchen at home.
13. He likes a / the kitchen in this house a lot.
14. A / The refrigerator is large and modern.
15. A / The house has a nice dining room next to a / the kitchen.
16. There are two bathrooms. A / The bathroom on a / the first floor is small.
17. A / The bathroom on a / the second floor is very large.
18. There's only one problem with a / the house: An / The owner wants a lot of money for it.

3 | **A, AN, OR THE** • *Complete the conversation with* **a, an,** *or* **the.**

AGENT: Do you like _____the_____ house?
                                    1.

ISABEL: Oh, very much. We need _____ house with _____ office.
                                        2.   **3.**

AGENT: _____ office is very nice. There's enough room for _____
                4.   **5.**
big desk and _____ couch.
                    6.

HUGO: And _____ kitchen is great! It's nice and bright.
                    7.

AGENT: Yes. It gets _____ sun in _____ late afternoon.
                            8.   **9.**

HUGO: _____ refrigerator looks really good.
                10.

AGENT: It's new. _____ owner just bought it.
                        11.

ISABEL: Why does _____ owner want to move?
                            12.

AGENT: She's _____ widow—her husband died last year. She wants to
                    13.
be closer to her children. They own _____ business in Toronto.
                                            14.

HUGO: I see. Does _____ house have _____ fireplace?
                            15.   **16.**

AGENT: Yes. _____ fireplace is in _____ living room.
                    17.   **18.**
We saw it when we came in.

HUGO: Oh, that's right. I forgot. Can we see _____ garage?
                                                        19.

AGENT: Sure. Come with me.

4 | **EDIT** • *Read this ad. Find and correct ten mistakes in the use of* **a, an,** *and* **the.**
The first mistake is already corrected.

> # FIND ~~A~~ The HOME OF YOUR DREAMS
>
> *Realty of Dreams*
>
> **A**re you looking for the new home? The real estate
> agent can help you find the home of your dreams.
> A right agent can save you a lot of time—and money.
> Describe your dream home, and your agent will help you
> from the beginning to an end: from looking at your home for
> a first time, to finding a best moving company. We are a largest real estate agency
> in the country. We can help you find a best house for you. Call us at **555-HOME**.
> We have more than 100 agents. The agent will be happy to help you.

UNIT 21 — No Article (Ø) or *The*

1 NO ARCTICLE (Ø) OR THE • *Check the best answer.*

1. Andrea doesn't like coffee.
   - ☑ Andrea doesn't like any kind of coffee.
   - ❏ Andrea doesn't like this coffee.

2. The coffee is very strong.
   - ❏ All coffee is very strong.
   - ❏ This coffee is very strong.

3. The students study hard.
   - ❏ All students study hard.
   - ❏ These students study hard.

4. The music is loud.
   - ❏ All music is loud.
   - ❏ This music is loud.

5. He sings her songs in concerts.
   - ❏ He sings them in a lot of concerts.
   - ❏ He's singing them in this concert.

6. I like the songs.
   - ❏ I like all songs.
   - ❏ I like these songs.

2 NO ARTICLE (Ø) OR THE • *Circle the correct words.*

1. **A:** Let's go to mall / (the mall.)

   B: OK. I need clothes / the clothes.

2. **A:** Clothes / The clothes at Maxi's are nice.

   B: And salespeople / the salespeople are very helpful.

3. **A:** Do you like these?

   B: No. I never wear jeans / the jeans. I prefer skirts / the skirts.

4. **A:** The T-shirts / T-shirts at Maxi's are great.

   B: The prices / Prices there are great too.

5. **A:** I don't like this store. Music / The music is too loud.

   B: Let's take a break and go to cafeteria / the cafeteria.

6. **A:** How's coffee / the coffee?

   B: I usually don't drink coffee / the coffee, but this isn't bad.

7. **A:** Do you go to concerts / the concerts?

   B: Sometimes. Why? Do you have tickets / the tickets?

8. **A:** I wanted to go to concert / the concert.

   B: Me too. But tickets / the tickets were too expensive.

3 **NO ARTICLE (Ø) OR THE • Complete with the when necessary.**

1. **A:** Does your teacher give you _____—_____ homework every day?

   B: Yes, and I didn't finish _____the_____ homework for today.

2. **A:** Did you understand _____ last problem?

   B: No. Of course not! You know, _____ math isn't my best subject.

3. **A:** What kinds of food do you like? Do you like _____ pizza?

   B: Yes. I love _____ pizza. But I don't like _____ pizza

   in _____ school cafeteria!

4. **A:** Do you enjoy _____ sports?

   B: I love _____ sports, but _____ soccer is my favorite game.

5. **A:** _____ game last Saturday was really terrific.

   B: I heard _____ teams played really well.

6. **A:** You know, _____ tennis is very popular in my school.

   B: I love _____ tennis.

7. **A:** Did you take _____ tennis lessons?

   B: Yes. I was a member of _____ school tennis club.

8. **A:** Let's go to _____ game tomorrow night.

   B: I can't. I'm going to go to _____ school concert.

9. **A:** I love _____ music. Who's going to play?

   B: I can't remember _____ name of _____ group. But

   _____ people say _____ singer is great.

10. **A:** Let's get _____ ice cream after _____ concert.

    B: Good idea. We can go to _____ ice cream shop on Main Street.

11. **A:** Mmm. This is good. Would you like to try it?

    B: No, thanks. I don't like _____ chocolate ice cream.

12. **A:** It's getting late. _____ bus leaves in ten minutes.

    B: OK. I'll ask for _____ check.

UNIT 22

Quantifiers: *Some* and *Any*

1 **AFFIRMATIVE AND NEGATIVE STATEMENTS** • *Complete the sentences with* **some** *or* **any**.

1. There aren't ____any____ stamps.
2. I want to send _____ letters.
3. There's _____ mail in the mailbox.
4. We don't have _____ paper for the printer.
5. I brought Ellen _____ flowers for her birthday.
6. They're beautiful! I'll put them in _____ water right now.
7. I saw _____ nice shoes at the mall.
8. They didn't have _____ shoes in my size.
9. I'm thirsty. I'm going to get _____ soda from the refrigerator.
10. There isn't _____ soda, but there's _____ cold water.
11. Do we have _____ ice?
12. I invited _____ friends for dinner.
13. Are there _____ clean glasses?

2 **QUESTIONS AND ANSWERS** • *Complete the conversations with* **some** *or* **any** *and the correct form of the words in parentheses.*

A: Do we have _____any fruit_____?
　　　　　　　　　　　 1. (fruit)

B: There are _____some apples_____, but there aren't _____.
　　　　　　　　　 2. (apples) 　　　　　　　　　　　 **3. (banana)**

A: Do you have _____ tonight?
　　　　　　　　　 4. (homework)

B: No, but I have _____ next week, so I'm going to study.
　　　　　　　　　　　　 5. (test)

A: Do we have _____?
　　　　　　　　　 6. (coffee)

B: I forgot to buy coffee. Would you like _____?
　　　　　　　　　　　　　　　　　　　　　 7. (tea)

A: Could I have _____?
　　　　　　　　 8. (ice cream)

B: Sure. We have _____ in the refrigerator.
　　　　　　　　　 9. (chocolate ice cream)

A: Are there _____?
　　　　　　　 10. (nuts)

3 **STATEMENTS AND QUESTIONS** • Complete the sentences with **some** or **any** and the correct form of a word from the box.

cookie	cup	electricity	~~food~~
furniture	photo	snow	student

1. Let's go to the grocery store. There isn't _____any food_____ in the house.

2. Do they have _____ at the flea market? I need a table.

3. Last winter was warm. We didn't get _____ .

4. The kitchen smells great. We just baked _____ .

5. How's your new camera? Did you take _____ good _____ on your trip?

6. All the lights went out. We didn't have _____ after the storm.

7. There are _____ from Brazil in our language class.

8. I'm making coffee. Are there _____ clean _____ ?

4 **AFFIRMATIVE AND NEGATIVE STATEMENTS** • Look at the things Mai planned to get yesterday. The things she got are checked (✓). Complete the paragraph about the things she did and didn't do. Use **some** or **any**.

Mai went to the mall today. She didn't buy _____any shirts_____ there, but she
                                              1.
got _____ nice _____. Then she went to the post office.
                        2.
She mailed _____. She didn't get _____ because the line was
              3.   **4.**
very long. At the video store, they didn't have _____ new _____,
                                                                    5.
so she rented _____. Last, Mai went to the grocery store and bought
                  6.
_____ for breakfast. She was tired, so she didn't buy _____ or
  7.   **8.**
_____ for dinner. She went home, ordered a pizza, and watched a movie!
  9.

Quantifiers: *Many, Much, A few, A little, A lot of*

1 **QUANTIFIERS** • *Check the quantifiers you can use with these nouns.*

	MANY	MUCH	A FEW	A LITTLE	A LOT OF
1. books	✔		✔		✔
2. water					
3. time					
4. friends					
5. people					
6. work					
7. tests					
8. music					
9. CDs					
10. movies					

2 **STATEMENTS** • *Circle the correct words to complete the sentences.*

1. Kayla has <u>a lot of</u> / much friends.

2. She doesn't have <u>many / much</u> free time.

3. She spends <u>many / much</u> hours in the library.

4. She always has <u>a lot of / many</u> homework.

5. How <u>many / much</u> hours does she study?

6. She studies <u>a few / a little</u> hours every morning.

7. Sometimes she listens to <u>a few / a little</u> music when she studies.

8. Her teacher gives <u>a few / a little</u> tests every month.

9. The tests have <u>much / many</u> questions.

10. Kayla sometimes gets <u>a few / a little</u> answers wrong.

11. She doesn't get <u>much / many</u> bad grades.

12. In class, they talk about <u>many / much</u> interesting things.

13. <u>Many / Much</u> students want to take the class.

14. Kayla enjoys the class <u>a lot of / a lot</u>.

15. The classes are <u>a lot of / a lot</u> fun.

3 **STATEMENTS** • *Look at the picture. Complete the sentences with* **many**, **much**, **a few**, **a little**, *or* **a lot of**. *Use* **not** *when necessary. Sometimes more than one answer is correct.*

1. There is ___n't much___ paper on the desk.
2. There are _____ dictionaries on the desk.
3. There are _____ books on the shelf.
4. There are _____ photos on the desk.
5. There are _____ bottles of water.
6. There is _____ water in the bottles.
7. There is _____ paper in the waste basket.
8. There are _____ pens on the desk.
9. There are _____ flowers in the vase.
10. There is _____ water in the vase.

4 **QUESTIONS AND ANSWERS** • *Complete the questions with* **How much** *or* **How many**. *Answer the questions with* **many**, **much**, **a few**, **a little**, **a lot**, *or* **a lot of**. *Sometimes more than one answer is correct.*

1. **A:** ___How much___ homework do you have tonight?

   B: ___A few___ hours. Maybe one or two.

2. **A:** _____ friends does Kyle have?

   B: Oh. He has _____ friends. He's very popular.

3. **A:** _____ books do you read every year?

   B: Only _____. I don't have _____ free time.

4. **A:** _____ money does Marta save every year?

   B: I think she saves _____. She's going to buy a new car this month.

5. **A:** _____ people did you invite to your party?

   B: I invited _____ people! I hope there's enough room!

6. **A:** _____ time do you spend on the phone?

   B: Only _____. I don't like to talk on the phone.

7. **A:** _____ water do you drink every day?

   B: _____! More than eight glasses.

8. **A:** _____ times did you see Todd last year?

   B: Just _____. We were both very busy.

UNIT 24 There is, There are

1 **AFFIRMATIVE STATEMENTS** • *Complete the sentences with* **there is**, **there are**, **there was**, **there were**, *or* **there will be**.

1. _____There were_____ a lot of people at the restaurant yesterday.
2. Taste the soup. I think _____ too much salt in it.
3. _____ five people at tomorrow's meeting.
4. _____ too many mistakes in this report. Please correct them.
5. _____ time to correct them tomorrow.
6. _____ an accident in front of the school yesterday morning.
7. _____ a lot of police officers at the scene of yesterday's accident.
8. Here's the paper. _____ an interesting article on page 5.

2 **NEGATIVE STATEMENTS** • *Complete the sentences with* **there is**, **there are**, **there isn't**, **there aren't**, **there wasn't**, **there weren't**, *or* **there won't be**.

1. _____There weren't_____ many people at yesterday's meeting.
2. _____ any classes tomorrow because of the storm.
3. _____ any coffee in the pot. Can you please make some more?
4. We have a lot of bananas, but _____ any apples.
5. _____ no milk. Could you please buy some on your way home?
6. I didn't call Sara. _____ enough time.
7. _____ no knives on the table. Could you get some?
8. I have to finish my paper today. _____ enough time to do it tomorrow.

3 **WH- QUESTIONS** • *Read the answers and then ask questions about the underlined words.*

1. **Q:** _How many students are there?_____
   A: There are <u>twenty</u> students.
2. **Q:** _____
   A: There's <u>a bottle of</u> soda.
3. **Q:** _____
   A: There were <u>ten</u> tables.

4. Q: _____

A: There will be <u>100</u> people.

5. Q: _____

A: There will be <u>a lot of</u> time.

---

4 **YES/NO QUESTIONS AND SHORT ANSWERS** • *Look at the list of supplies. Complete the questions and write short answers.*

> ## Supplies
>
> butter ✔   salt ✔
>
> milk   sugar
>
> bananas   bread ✔
>
> tomatoes ✔   spaghetti
>
> lemons ✔   rice

1. Q: <u>Is there any</u> _____ butter?

A: <u>Yes, there is.</u> _____

2. Q: _____ milk?

A: _____

3. Q: _____ bananas?

A: _____

4. Q: _____ tomatoes?

A: _____

5. Q: _____ lemons?

A: _____

6. Q: _____ salt?

A: _____

7. Q: _____ sugar?

A: _____

8. Q: _____ bread?

A: _____

9. Q: _____ spaghetti?

A: _____

10. Q: _____ rice?

A: _____

SelfTest

SECTION ONE

Circle the letter of the correct answer to complete each sentence.

EXAMPLE: Carlos _____ a student.	**A B ⓒ D**
(A) are (C) is	
(B) does (D) were	

1. Did you take _____ tests last week? **A B C D**
   (A) ones (C) a little
   (B) much (D) a lot of

2. My shoes _____ too small. **A B C D**
   (A) are (C) is
   (B) be (D) am

3. —There isn't any milk in the fridge. **A B C D**
   —I'll go buy _____.
   (A) any (C) some
   (B) much (D) a few

4. I'm going to be late. There's _____ traffic. **A B C D**
   (A) many (C) a few
   (B) a lot (D) a lot of

5. —What do you want to be after college? **A B C D**
   —_____ accountant.
   (A) A (C) Some
   (B) An (D) The

6. I bought some soda. Would you like _____ can? **A B C D**
   (A) a (C) some
   (B) the (D) any

7. Did you find _____ interesting things at the market? **A B C D**
   (A) much (C) this
   (B) any (D) a little

8. —What does Marisa do? **A B C D**
   —She writes _____ articles for a big newspaper.
   (A) the (C) Ø
   (B) an (D) any

9. Where is _____ kitchen in this apartment? **A B C D**
   (A) a (C) Ø
   (B) the (D) one

10. Would you like a cup _____ coffee? **A B C D**
    (A) Ø (C) the
    (B) some (D) of

11. I'll meet you in front of _____ library tomorrow. **A B C D**
    (A) a   (C) Ø
    (B) the   (D) some

12. We bought _____ CDs at the market. **A B C D**
    (A) a few   (C) much
    (B) a lot   (D) a

SECTION TWO

Each sentence has four underlined parts. The four underlined parts are marked A, B, C, and D. Circle the letter of the part that is NOT CORRECT.

> **EXAMPLE:**
>
> Carla <u>is</u> a student, but she <u>are</u> <u>not</u> in school <u>today</u>.   A Ⓑ C D
>   A   B C   D

13. There <u>are</u> twenty <u>children</u> in Mr. <u>Lin's</u> class this <u>Year</u>. **A B C D**
          A   B   C   D

14. Two <u>woman</u> at <u>Alicia's</u> party last <u>week</u> were <u>lawyers</u>. **A B C D**
         A   B   C   D

15. I read *Far Tower*, and I liked <u>the</u> <u>story</u>, but I didn't like <u>movie</u>. **A B C D**
            A   B C   D

16. My <u>doctor</u> says I shouldn't drink eight <u>cups</u> <u>of</u> <u>coffees</u> every day. **A B C D**
      A   B C D

17. Sam is <u>a</u> engineer, and his <u>wife</u> is <u>the</u> president of <u>ABC</u>, Inc. **A B C D**
         A   B   C   D

18. My <u>friend</u> <u>Yuki</u> moved to <u>brazil</u> last <u>year</u>. **A B C D**
      A   B   C   D

19. Ty's <u>sister</u> <u>Sara</u> wants to go to <u>an</u> university in <u>Canada</u>. **A B C D**
       A   B   C   D

20. <u>I</u> saw <u>the</u> good <u>show</u> on TV, but I don't remember its <u>name</u>. **A B C D**
  A   B   C   D

21. Harrods <u>are</u> a big department <u>store</u> in <u>London</u>, <u>England</u>. **A B C D**
        A   B   C   D

22. We went to <u>the</u> <u>market</u> on D <u>Street</u>, but we didn't buy <u>a lot of</u>. **A B C D**
           A   B   C   D

23. I went to the <u>store</u> and bought <u>a pair of</u> <u>short</u> and some <u>jeans</u>. **A B C D**
          A   B   C   D

24. Would you like <u>a</u> <u>cup tea</u> and <u>some</u> <u>cookies</u>? **A B C D**
               A B   C   D

25. I didn't pack <u>many</u> <u>clothes</u>, but I brought <u>much</u> <u>books</u>. **A B C D**
          A   B   C   D

Pronouns:
Subject and Object

---

1   **SUBJECT AND OBJECT PRONOUNS** • *Complete with the correct pronouns.*

SUBJECT	OBJECT
I	me
_____	you
he	_____
she	_____
it	_____
_____	us
you	_____
_____	them

2   **SUBJECT AND OBJECT PRONOUNS** • *Circle the correct pronouns to complete Doug's diary entry.*

Yesterday was my birthday. My friend Toby gave I / (me) a party. It / They was
1.   **2.**

great. I / Me had a really good time. A lot of my classmates came. It was good
3.

to see they / them. Megan was there too. I like she / her a lot. She / Her is a very
4.   **5.**   **6.**

good friend. I / me got a lot of nice presents. Megan gave I / me a sweater. He's / It's
7.   **8.**   **9.**

red. I showed it / him to my parents, and they / them said it / he looks great on I / me.
10.   **11.**   **12.**   **13.**

Next week is Megan's birthday. I want to get she / her a nice present too.
14.

3   **SUBJECT AND OBJECT PRONOUNS** • *Rewrite these sentences. Use pronouns in place of the underlined words.*

1. <u>My sister</u> invited <u>Mr. Rodriguez</u>. *She invited him.* _____
2. <u>The children</u> played with <u>the toy</u>. _____
3. <u>His uncle</u> baked <u>two cakes</u>. _____
4. <u>Her aunt</u> gave <u>the present</u> to <u>her niece Jenna</u>. _____
5. <u>Jenna</u> loved <u>the present</u>. _____

62

6. The blouse looked great on Jenna. _____

7. Did your brother like the party too? _____

8. My brother sat between the man and the woman. _____

9. I sent an e-mail to my sister. _____

10. Did you give the presents to the children? _____

11. The woman told my brother about the movie. _____

12. My brother recommended the movie to my aunt. _____

4   **SUBJECT AND OBJECT PRONOUNS • *Complete the conversation with the correct pronouns.***

MOTHER: The phone is ringing. Could you answer _____it_____? _____'s
    1.   2.
    probably for _____!
                 3.

MEGAN: Sure. _____'ll get _____. . . . Hello?
              4.   5.

DOUG: Hi, Megan. It's _____.
                      6.

MEGAN: Hi, Doug. How are _____?
                         7.

DOUG: Great. And _____?
                 8.

MEGAN: Good. That was a great party. I really enjoyed _____.
                                                       9.
    _____ was a lot of fun.
    10.

DOUG: _____ want to thank _____ again for the sweater.
      11.   12.
    _____ love _____.
    13.   14.

MEGAN: You're welcome. _____ looks great on _____.
                       15.   16.
    Hey, are _____ busy Friday night? Lila and _____ are
             17.   18.
    going to the movies. Would _____ like to come with _____?
                               19.   20.

DOUG: Sure. What time does _____ start?
                           21.

MEGAN: _____ starts at 10:00.
       22.

DOUG: What about Carlos and Eva? Can we invite _____ too?
                                               23.

MEGAN: Sure, but _____ think _____'re busy Friday night.
                 24.   25.
    _____'ll call Eva and ask _____. Maybe _____'m wrong.
    26.   27.   28.

DOUG: OK. Call _____ again after you talk to _____.
               29.   30.

MEGAN: OK. _____'ll call _____ later. Bye.
           31.   32.

Possessives

UNIT 26

---

1 **POSSESSIVES** • *Put these words in the correct column. Some words go in more than one column.*

our	hers	her	his	mine	the man's	yours
Marta's	my	their	the girls'	your	theirs	ours

THIS IS _____ HAT.

our

_____

_____

_____

_____

_____

_____

_____

THIS HAT IS _____.

hers

_____

_____

_____

_____

_____

_____

_____

2 **POSSESSIVES** • *Circle the letter of the correct answers.*

1. _____ book is on the table.
   a. Jon
   b. Jon's

2. _____ book is that?
   a. Who
   b. Whose

3. It's _____ book.
   a. her
   b. hers

4. It isn't _____.
   a. my
   b. mine

5. _____ is black.
   a. Our
   b. Ours

6. Maybe it's _____.
   a. their
   b. theirs

7. Is this _____?
   a. my
   b. mine

8. It's _____ home.
   a. their
   b. theirs

9. My _____ coat is blue.
   a. sister
   b. sister's

10. _____ house is beautiful.
   a. Your
   b. Yours

3 **WORD ORDER •** *Put the words in the correct order to make statements or questions.*

1. is • hat • whose • that

   _Whose hat is that_____?

2. not • my • that's • hat

   _____.

3. isn't • hat • white • my

   _____.

4. hat • that's • Natalie's

   _____.

5. white • hat • is • her

   _____?

6. it • hers • isn't

   _____.

7. is • smaller • hers

   _____.

8. this • whose • is

   _____?

9. mother's • that's • my • hat

   _____.

4 **POSSESSIVES •** *Complete the conversations with the correct possessive. Sometimes more than one answer is correct.*

1. **JASON:** Is this ___your___ bag, Mai?
                        a.

   MAI: No. _____ bag is gray. Maybe it's _____. _____ is white.
                  b.   **c.**   **d.**

2. **JASON:** Is the white bag _____, Todd?
                                a.

   TODD: Yes, it's _____. Thanks.
                       b.

3. **JASON:** Which bag belongs to Mai?

   LISA: I think the white one is _____.
                                      a.

   HENRI: No, it isn't. The gray one is _____ bag.
                                            b.

4. **JASON:** Which bag belongs to Henri and Lisa?

   MAI: I think the black one is _____. Right, Lisa? Henri?
                                     a.

   LISA: You're right. The black one is _____ bag.
                                            b.

   HENRI: Yes. The black one is _____.
                                    c.

UNIT 27   This, That, These, Those

---

1   **STATEMENTS WITH THIS OR THAT** • *Complete these sentences with* **this** *or* **that**.

1. Sorry. ___That___ is not my bag over there.
2. Mmm. _____ cake is delicious. Here, try some.
3. Look at _____ building over there.
4. Hi, Rod? _____ is Joachim. How are you?
5. Dania, _____ is my good friend, Molly. Molly, _____ is Dania.
6. Thank you! _____ is a wonderful gift. I love it!
7. _____ is my suitcase. See? Here's my name on it.
8. _____ looks like my teacher across the street!

2   **STATEMENTS WITH THESE OR THOSE** • *Complete these sentences with* **these** *or* **those**.

1. Here. Try one of ___these___ cookies. They're delicious.
2. Please hand me _____ books. I can't reach them.
3. Look at _____ people across the street.
4. _____ are my bags over there.
5. Please take _____ boxes from me. They're too heavy.
6. Here. _____ are our passports.
7. _____ are the Alps in the distance.
8. Let's change seats. _____ aren't good. I can't see.

3   **STATEMENTS WITH THIS, THAT, THESE OR THOSE** • *Complete these conversations with* **this, that, these,** *or* **those**.

1. **A:** Sara, ___this___ is my friend Anton.
       a.
   B: Hi, Anton. Nice to meet you. _____ are my parents.
                                          b.
   A: Nice to meet you.

2. **A:** _____ cookies are delicious. Here, have one.
          a.
   B: Thanks. _____ cake is great too. Here, try some.
                  b.

3. **A:** I bought _____ jeans, but they're too tight.
                    a.
   B: I think they look good on you. And _____ sweater looks great too.
                                             b.

66

4. A: [*phone rings*] Hi, Toby? _____ is Ina.
　　　　　　　　　　　　　　　　　a.

　B: Hi, Ina. _____ isn't Toby. _____ is Lee.
　　　　　　　b.　　　　　　　　**c.**

5. A: I can't reach _____ glasses on the top shelf.
　　　　　　　　　　　　　a.

　B: Here they are. _____ are pretty. Where did you get them?
　　　　　　　　　　　b.

6. A: Look across the street. _____ looks like Mr. Rodriguez.
　　　　　　　　　　　　　　　　a.

　B: _____ isn't Mr. Rodriguez. He's too short.
　　　　b.

7. A: Look! _____ are the Pyrenees in the distance.
　　　　　　　a.

　B: Look at them through _____ binoculars. You can see them better.
　　　　　　　　　　　　　　　b.

8. A: Let's walk over to _____ bookstore.
　　　　　　　　　　　　a.

　B: OK. Then I'd like to take a look at _____ flowers over there.
　　　　　　　　　　　　　　　　　　　b.

9. A: Wow! _____ bookstore is great!
　　　　　　　a.

　B: _____ prices are great too. _____ book here only costs $1.00.
　　　　b.　　　　　　　　　　**c.**

10. A: I'm thirsty. Let's go to _____ café over there.
　　　　　　　　　　　　　　　a.

　B: Good idea. Give me _____ bag there. I'll carry it for you. It looks heavy.
　　　　　　　　　　　b.

4　**QUESTIONS AND SHORT ANSWERS •** *Complete the questions with* **this, that, these,** *and* **those**
and the correct form of the verb **be***. Write short answers.*

1. A: _____Are those_____ your books over there?

　B: _No, they aren't_ . Mine are right here.

2. A: _____ Ms. Chen across the street?

　B: _____. Let's go say hello to her.

3. A: _____ your CDs here?

　B: _____. Thanks! I almost forgot them.

4. A: _____ your bag? It's very heavy.

　B: _____. Here. Give it to me. I'll carry it.

5. A: _____ the Himalayas in the distance?

　B: _____. Wow! They're beautiful!

6. A: [*phone rings*] Hello?

　B: _____ Marsha Thompson?

　A: _____. How can I help you?

UNIT 28 — One, Ones

 1 **STATEMENTS •** *Look at the pictures. Circle the correct words to complete the sentences.*

1. I like the big (one)/ ones.

2. I'll get the gray one / ones.

3. I prefer the one / ones on the right.

4. The one / ones in the middle is nice.

5. Wear the one / ones on the right.

6. These cookies are good. Try one / ones.

2 **QUESTIONS •** *Ask questions with* **Which one** *or* **Which ones**.

1. **A:** I'd like to try on some pants.

   B: _____ Which ones? _____

2. **A:** I'm going to buy one of those watches.

   B: _____

3. **A:** One of the elevators is broken.

   B: _____

4. **A:** Can I see those earrings over there?

   B: _____

5. **A:** I think I'll get some of these T-shirts.

   B: _____

6. **A:** Can I borrow one of your sweaters?

   B: _____

3 QUESTIONS AND ANSWERS • Complete the conversations with one and ones.

1. **A:** I need a salesperson. Do you see ___one___?
   a.

   B: There's _____ over there, but he's busy.
   b.

2. **A:** Can I help you?

   B: Yes. I'm looking for a sweater. This _____ is nice. Do you have it in black?
   a.

   A: Sorry. That _____ comes in white or gray only.
   b.

3. **A:** Those are nice shoes.

   B: Which _____?
   a.

   A: The brown _____.
   b.

   B: Oh. I think I prefer the black _____.
   c.

   A: Try them both on.

   B: OK. Hmmm. The black _____ feel a little too tight. The brown shoes
   d.

   are more comfortable, but the left _____ is a little too big.
   e.

4. **A:** Did you see those great paintings at the art show?

   B: Which _____? There were a lot of nice _____.
   a.   b.

   A: The _____ near the front door. I bought _____.
   c.   d.

   B: Really? Which _____?
   e.

   A: The _____ with the blue vase and yellow flowers.
   f.

   B: I remember that _____! It was my favorite of all the _____ there.
   g.   h.

4 EDIT • Read this e-mail message. Find and correct six mistakes in the use of one and ones. The first mistake is already corrected.

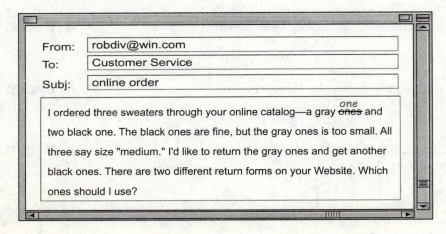

From: robdiv@win.com
To: Customer Service
Subj: online order

I ordered three sweaters through your online catalog—a gray ~~ones~~ *one* and
two black one. The black ones are fine, but the gray ones is too small. All
three say size "medium." I'd like to return the gray ones and get another
black ones. There are two different return forms on your Website. Which
ones should I use?

SelfTest

SECTION ONE

Circle the letter of the correct answer to complete each sentence.

EXAMPLE: Carlos _____ a student.   A B Ⓒ D
    (A) are   (C) is
    (B) does   (D) were

1. I wrote _____ a letter.   A B C D
    (A) they   (C) their
    (B) them   (D) theirs

2. _____ sent me an e-mail.   A B C D
    (A) They   (C) Their
    (B) Them   (D) Theirs

3. I spoke to _____ and her brother at the party.   A B C D
    (A) she   (C) her
    (B) she's   (D) hers

4. _____ book is that?   A B C D
    (A) Who's   (C) Whose
    (B) Where   (D) When

5. This is _____ homework.   A B C D
    (A) me   (C) mine
    (B) my   (D) of me

6. Where's John? This is _____ coat.   A B C D
    (A) John   (C) Johns'
    (B) John's   (D) John his

7. The sweater isn't _____.   A B C D
    (A) she   (C) hers
    (B) her   (D) she's

8. Could you hand me _____ bag over there?   A B C D
    (A) this   (C) these
    (B) that   (D) those

9. _____ cookies are delicious. Here, try one.   A B C D
    (A) This   (C) These
    (B) That   (D) Those

10. —Jason, _____ is Alicia.   A B C D
    —Nice to meet you, Alicia.
    (A) she   (C) it
    (B) that   (D) this

11. —Is this your passport?
    —Yes, _____.
    (A) this is   (C) it is
    (B) that is   (D) it's

A B C D

12. —Can I borrow a book?
    —Sure. Which _____ do you want?
    (A) it   (C) them
    (B) one   (D) ones

A B C D

13. _____ movie did you like better?
    (A) Who   (C) How
    (B) Where   (D) Which

A B C D

SECTION TWO

Each sentence or pair of sentences has four underlined parts. The four underlined parts are marked A, B, C, and D. Circle the letter of the part that is NOT CORRECT.

EXAMPLE:

Carla <u>is</u> a student, but she <u>are</u> <u>not</u> in school <u>today</u>.
   A   B   C   D

A (B) C D

14. <u>This</u> is the lake, <u>that's</u> the boat, and <u>those</u> man is <u>our</u> guide.
    A   B   C   D

A B C D

15. <u>These</u> reports <u>are</u> good, but <u>yours</u> is the best <u>ones</u>.
    A   B   C   D

A B C D

16. <u>My</u> <u>cousin he</u> called <u>me</u> and told me about <u>his</u> new job.
    A   B   C   D

A B C D

17. <u>That one</u> over there is <u>yours</u>, but <u>this one</u> here is <u>Megan</u>.
    A   B   C   D

A B C D

18. Is <u>that</u> <u>yours</u> jacket or is it <u>your</u> <u>sister's</u>?
      A   B   C   D

A B C D

19. <u>This</u> isn't <u>my</u> bag, but <u>that</u> two over there are <u>mine</u>.
    A   B   C   D

A B C D

20. <u>I</u> forgot <u>my</u> pen. Can I borrow <u>ones</u> of <u>yours</u>?
   A   B   C   D

A B C D

21. <u>Those</u> T-shirts <u>are</u> nice. I'd like to get <u>ones</u> for <u>my</u> brother.
    A   B   C   D

A B C D

22. <u>It</u> <u>was</u> a beautiful day, and <u>my</u> sister enjoyed <u>its</u> a lot.
   A B   C   D

A B C D

23. <u>Kevin's</u> grades were good, but <u>his</u> <u>brother</u> <u>were</u> not.
    A   B   C   D

A B C D

24. <u>Whose</u> <u>one</u> do you want—the red <u>one</u> or the blue <u>one</u>?
    A   B   C   D

A B C D

25. <u>He</u> offered <u>her</u> <u>his</u> soup, but she already had <u>one</u>.
    A   B C   D

A B C D

Adjectives

1 **MEANING** • *Match each adjective with the correct category.*

ADJECTIVE

_____h___ **1.** big

_____ **2.** square

_____ **3.** angry

_____ **4.** blue

_____ **5.** cold

_____ **6.** pretty

_____ **7.** friendly

_____ **8.** old

_____ **9.** Canadian

CATEGORY

a. Age

b. Appearance

c. Color

d. Feelings

e. Nationality

f. Personality

g. Shape

h. Size

i. Temperature

2 **WORD ORDER** • *Put the words in the correct order.*

1. small • house • is • Their
   Their house is small.

2. big • has • garden • a • It
   _____

3. kitchen • sunny • There's • a
   _____

4. comfortable • looks • The • living room
   _____

5. large • bedroom • seems • The
   _____

6. have • They • office • a • nice
   _____

7. is • cute • Their • cat
   _____

8. a • She's • cat • friendly
   _____

3 **MEANING AND WORD ORDER** • *Complete these sentences with the correct adjectives and nouns from the boxes.*

cool	crowded	h~~o~~t	beach	d~~a~~y	water

1. It's a ___hot___ ___day___ . The temperature is over 90°F (32°C).
2. The _____ is _____. There are a lot of people on the sand.
3. Paulo is swimming in the ocean. He's enjoying the _____ _____.

beautiful	large	expensive	new	clothes	mall	sweater

4. Laura is shopping in a _____ _____. She's looking in a lot of stores.
5. She's looking for some _____ _____ for school.
6. She sees a _____ _____. She really likes it.
7. How much is it? It looks _____.

English	good	Mexican	class	student	teacher

8. Ana Rivera is a _____ _____ from Guadalajara.
9. She's in my _____ _____ at the university.
10. Our _____ is _____. We learn a lot from him.

4 **EDIT** • *Read this journal entry. Find and correct seven mistakes in the use of adjectives. The first mistake is already corrected.*

✿ ✿ ✿ ✿ ✿

    I like my ~~class English~~. *English class* The teacher is very good, and the students friendly are. Our classroom is very pleasant too. It's not a room big, but it's sunny and has comfortables chairs. There's only one problem—it sometimes gets hotly. We can't open the windows because then it's noisy.

    Tomorrow we are going on a class trip. I hope it's a day hot because we're going to the beach. There are some beautifuls beaches near the school. I can wear my new swimsuit. Janna says the water is great. That's good news. I want to go swimming!

Comparisons: *As . . . as*

1 **MEANING** • *Look at the pictures. Circle the letter of the correct description.*

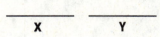

1. a. X is as tall as Y.
   b. X isn't as tall as Y.
   c. Y isn't as tall as X. *(circled)*

2. a. X is as long as Y.
   b. X isn't as long as Y.
   c. Y isn't as long as X.

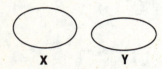

3. a. X is as big as Y.
   b. X isn't as big as Y.
   c. Y isn't as big as X.

4. a. X is as dark as Y.
   b. X isn't as dark as Y.
   c. Y isn't as dark as X.

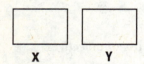

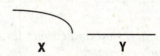

5. a. X is as wide as Y.
   b. X isn't as wide as Y.
   c. Y isn't as wide as X.

6. a. X is as straight as Y.
   b. X isn't as straight as Y.
   c. Y isn't as straight as X.

2 **AFFIRMATIVE AND NEGATIVE** • *Look at the chart. Complete the sentences on the next page with* **as** + *adjective* + **as** *or* **not as** + *adjective* + **as**. *Use the adjectives in parentheses.*

	Megan	Josef	Anila
Age	17	17	18
Height	5'3"	5'4"	5'4"
Weight	124 lbs	115 lbs	120 lbs
Average Grade	A	A	B+

1. Megan is _____not as old as_____ Anila.
   (old)
2. Megan is _____ Josef.
   (old)
3. Josef is _____ Anila.
   (old)
4. Megan is _____ Josef or Anila.
   (tall)
5. Josef is _____ Anila.
   (tall)
6. Josef and Anila are _____ Megan.
   (short)
7. Josef is _____ Anila.
   (heavy)
8. Anila is _____ Megan.
   (heavy)
9. Anila's grades are _____ Josef's or Megan's.
   (good)
10. Josef's grades are _____ Megan's.
    (good)

3 **AFFIRMATIVE AND NEGATIVE •** *Complete these sentences with the correct form of* **be** *and* **(not)**
   as + *adjective* + **as** *or* **(not) as** + *adjective. Choose the correct adjectives from the box.*

| athletic | big | busy | expensive | ~~far~~ |
| good | happy | old | popular | tall |

1. Maria lives only five minutes from school. Eduardo lives a half an hour away.
   Maria's home ___isn't as far as___ Eduardo's.
2. Maria's rent is $400 a month. Eduardo's rent is $300. His rent _____.
3. His building has ten floors. Hers has two. Her building _____ his.
4. Maria has class five days a week. She also has a part-time job. Eduardo has class
   only on Tuesdays and Thursdays. Eduardo _____.
5. Eduardo gets all A's. Maria gets some B's. Maria's grades _____.
6. Maria and Eduardo both have five brothers and sisters. Maria's family
   _____ Eduardo's.
7. Eduardo is 21. Maria is only 19. Maria _____.
8. Maria is great at sports. Eduardo doesn't like sports. Eduardo _____.
9. Eduardo has a lot of friends at school. Maria has a lot of friends too.
   She _____ him.
10. Maria likes her life a lot. Eduardo likes his too. He _____ Maria.

UNIT 31 Comparative Adjectives

---

1   **SPELLING AND FORM** • *Complete with the correct comparative forms.*

ADJECTIVE	COMPARATIVE		ADJECTIVE	COMPARATIVE
1. tall	taller	8.	intelligent	_____
2. big	_____	9.	popular	_____
3. nice	_____	10.	short	_____
4. happy	_____	11.	pretty	_____
5. interesting	_____	12.	bad	_____
6. good	_____	13.	difficult	_____
7. strong	_____	14.	far	_____

2   **AFFIRMATIVE STATEMENTS** • *Look at the chart. Complete the statements with the comparative form of the correct adjective in parentheses. Circle the correct adjective.*

Portable CD Players

Brand	X	Y	Z
Price	$39.75	$159.99	$79.95
Weight	.37 lbs	.35 lbs	.34 lbs
Sound Quality	★★★	★★★★	★★★
Battery Life*	12 hrs	26 hrs	23 hrs

*the number of hours you can use the batteries

BATTERIES

1. Brand X is ___cheaper than___ Brand Y.
(**cheap** / expensive)

2. Brand Y is _____ Brand Z.
(cheap / expensive)

3. Brand Z is _____ Brand X.
(heavy / light)

4. Brand Y is _____ Brand Z.
(heavy / light)

5. The sound quality of Brand Y is _____ the sound quality of Brand X.
(good / bad)

6. The sound quality of Brand X is _____ the sound quality of Brand Y.
(good / bad)

7. The battery life of Brand X is _____ the battery life of Brand Y.
(short / long)

8. The battery life of Brand Y is _____ the battery life of Brand X.
(short / long)

3 **COMPARATIVES WITH THAN** • *Complete the sentences with the comparative form of the correct adjective from the box. Use* **than** *when necessary.*

athletic	difficult	easy	expensive	far
happy	~~old~~	strong	successful	tall

1. Jorge bought a CD player two years ago. I bought one last month. Jorge's CD player is __older than__ mine.

2. My TV cost $250. Jorge's cost $300. His TV is _____ mine.

3. Sara is good at sports, but her brother isn't. Sara is _____.

4. Todd is 6' tall. Max is 6'2". Max is _____.

5. I can lift a 25-lb weight. My sister can't. I'm _____ she is.

6. Lia is in Math 101. Her brother is in Math 102. Math 102 is _____.

7. Last year, the singer Natalie sold a million copies of her latest CD. The Blends sold 5 million. The Blends were _____ Natalie.

8. Megan's school is just around the corner from her home. Jenn has to take a bus to school. Jenn's school is _____.

9. Kriston smiles a lot. Amanda always looks sad. Kriston seems _____.

10. Bo gets A's on his math tests. Layla gets B's. Math is _____ for Bo.

4 **COMPARATIVES WITH THAN** • *Write sentences. Use the comparative with the correct form of* **be**.

1. Mustafa • tall • his brother __Mustafa is taller than his brother.__

2. The plane • fast • the train _____

3. The train • expensive • the bus _____

4. A monkey • intelligent • a dog _____

5. My grades • good • your grades _____

6. Tara • heavy • her sister _____

7. Calculus • difficult • algebra _____

8. Dina • happy • her brother _____

9. The bookstore • far • the café _____

10. The movie • bad • the book _____

11. Mexico City • hot • Paris _____

12. Luis • funny • Enrique _____

Superlative Adjectives

1 **SPELLING AND FORM** • *Complete with the correct superlative form.*

ADJECTIVE	SUPERLATIVE	ADJECTIVE	SUPERLATIVE
1. small	the smallest	9. spicy	_____
2. big	_____	10. fat	_____
3. funny	_____	11. cold	_____
4. interesting	_____	12. bad	_____
5. hot	_____	13. far	_____
6. good	_____	14. nice	_____
7. amazing	_____	15. important	_____
8. wonderful	_____	16. easy	_____

2 **SUPERLATIVE ADJECTIVES** • *Look at the chart. Complete the statements with the superlative form of the adjectives in parentheses. Write the Brand:* **X**, **Y**, *or* **Z**.

1. Brand ___X___ is ___the cheapest___ .
   (cheap)
2. Brand _____ is _____ .
   (expensive)
3. Brand _____ is _____ .
   (salty)
4. Brand _____ is _____ .
   (spicy)
5. Brand _____ is _____ .
   (sweet)
6. Brand _____ is _____ .
   (thick)
7. Brand _____ is _____ .
   (thin)
8. Brand _____ is _____ .
   (chunky)
9. Brand _____ has _____ taste.
   (good)
10. It's _____ of all.
    (delicious)

Spaghetti Sauce

less ◀———▶ more

Brand	X	Y	Z
Price	$1.30	$3.50	$1.50
Salty	○	●	◐
Spicy	●	◐	◐
Sweet	◐	○	●
Thick	○	●	◐
Chunky*	○	◐	●
Taste Quality	○	◐	●

*with pieces of tomato

3 **SUPERLATIVE ADJECTIVES** • *Complete the conversations with the superlative form of the correct adjectives from the box.*

| bad | cheap | delicious | dark | ~~good~~ |
| expensive | funny | long | old | popular |

1. **A:** Antonio's makes ___the best___ pizza. I love their sauce.

   B: But it's also _____. A slice costs more than $2.00.

2. **A:** Bruno's is _____ restaurant in town. Everyone goes there.

   B: It also has _____ lines. You always have to wait to get in.

3. **A:** The Tavern is _____ restaurant in town. It opened in 1726.

   B: It's also the _____! You can't see your food.

4. **A:** The Dock is _____ in town. I once got sick from its food.

   B: But it isn't _____. You pay a lot for bad food.

5. **A:** The Club has _____ waiters. I always laugh a lot there.

   B: And they have _____ desserts. I always get their chocolate cake.

4 **EDIT** • *Read this restaurant review. Find and correct eight mistakes in the use of the superlative. The first mistake is already corrected.*

❖ ❖ *Restaurant Review* ❖ ❖

    Last night I ate at the Florentine Grill. In a city with more than 100

restaurants, this is the ~~more~~ *most* beautiful restaurant in town. It's also the expensivest. I

was with a group of four people, and we each ordered something different. The

chicken with mushrooms and cream was definitely the deliciousest. The more

unusual dish was fish in a nut sauce. Very interesting. My wife likes spicy food. Her

spaghetti arrabiatta (in a hot pepper sauce) was the most hottest dish. (She almost

couldn't eat it.) My steak was good, but not the better. Desserts were terrific. They

make the good chocolate soufflé in the world!

    I recommend the Florentine Grill for a special event. Be sure to make a

reservation. This is one of the popularest restaurants in town.

UNIT 33 — Adjectives with *Very, Too,* and *Enough*

---

1 **WORD ORDER** • *Put these words in the correct order.*

1. very • road • is • dangerous • This   <u>This road is very dangerous.</u>
2. apartment • too • My • is • cold _____
3. grades • Her • enough • good • are _____
4. very • is • not • His • fast • car _____
5. is • The • not • strong • coffee • too _____
6. Our • not • enough • is • cheap • apartment _____
7. is • The • loud • music • too _____
8. enough • is • soup • salty • The _____

2 **MEANING** • *Circle the letter of the correct answer.*

1. I can't do my homework. It's _____.
   a. too easy   **b.** not difficult enough   **c.** too difficult *(circled)*

2. Could you please close the window? It's _____ in here.
   a. warm enough   **b.** too cold   **c.** not cold enough

3. We probably won't buy the car. It's _____.
   a. expensive enough   **b.** very expensive   **c.** not too expensive

4. I can't reach that top shelf. I'm not _____.
   a. short enough   **b.** tall enough   **c.** too short

5. Evan is only 13. He's _____ to drive a car.
   a. too old   **b.** old enough   **c.** not old enough

6. The cake is _____ good. Try some.
   a. too   **b.** very   **c.** enough

7. She's 25. She's not _____ to work.
   a. young enough   **b.** too young   **c.** very young

8. I can't fall asleep. The radio is _____.
   a. too loud   **b.** not loud enough   **c.** not too loud

9. Could you help me carry these boxes? They're _____ for me.
   a. heavy enough   **b.** not too heavy   **c.** too heavy

10. We couldn't buy tickets. They were _____.
    a. too cheap   **b.** very cheap   **c.** not cheap enough

80

3 **TOO OR ENOUGH** • *Complete these sentences with the adjectives in parentheses and* **too** *or* **enough**.

1. The motorcycle was ___too expensive___. She couldn't buy it.
   (expensive)
2. The suitcases were _____. I didn't need help with them.
   (light)
3. They didn't buy the house. It wasn't _____ for them.
   (big)
4. My grandfather can't drive now. He's _____.
   (old)
5. Put the coffee back in the microwave. It's not _____.
   (hot)
6. We didn't go to the beach. It wasn't _____.
   (warm)
7. They understood the movie. It wasn't _____.
   (difficult)
8. Please turn off the radio. It's _____.
   (loud)
9. Do you like the shoes? Are they _____?
   (comfortable)
10. I can't read my notes. It's _____ in here.
    (dark)
11. I didn't study last night. I was _____.
    (tired)
12. Sonia went back to school today. She felt _____.
    (well)
13. We didn't take the apartment. The rent wasn't _____.
    (cheap)
14. My sister can't drive. She's _____.
    (young)

4 **TOO, ENOUGH, OR VERY** • *Look at the picture. Describe the problems. Complete the sentences with the adjectives in parentheses. Use* **too**, **enough**, *or* **very**. *Sometimes more than one answer is possible.*

1. The carpet is ___too big OR very big___.
   (big)
2. The book shelves are _____.
   (high)
3. The closet isn't _____.
   (big)
4. The windows are _____.
   (dirty)
5. The couch isn't _____.
   (comfortable)
6. The plant isn't _____.
   (healthy)
7. The desk isn't _____.
   (neat)
8. The light is _____.
   (low)
9. The refrigerator is _____.
   (small)
10. In the winter the room isn't _____.
    (warm)

Adjectives and Adverbs

1 **SPELLING** • *Complete with the correct adjectives and adverbs.*

ADJECTIVES	ADVERBS	ADJECTIVES	ADVERBS
1. nice	*nicely*	**7.** easy	_____
2. _____	beautifully	**8.** _____	friendly
3. good	_____	**9.** fantastic	_____
4. quick	_____	**10.** _____	hard
5. _____	horribly	**11.** happy	_____
6. fast	_____	**12.** late	_____

2 **ADJECTIVE OR ADVERB** • *Circle the letter of the correct answer.*

1. They're _____ skaters.
   a. wonderful   **b.** wonderfully

2. They practice _____.
   a. hard   **b.** hardly

3. They're _____ learners.
   a. quick   **b.** quickly

4. We had a _____ time at the performance.
   a. great   **b.** greatly

5. We had _____ seats.
   a. terrific   **b.** terrifically

6. We could see very _____.
   a. good   **b.** well

7. Tania looked _____.
   a. beautiful   **b.** beautifully

8. She skated _____.
   a. perfect   **b.** perfectly

9. Her partner didn't skate _____.
   a. good   **b.** well

10. He seemed _____.
   a. unhappy   **b.** unhappily

3 **ADJECTIVE OR ADVERB** • *Complete these sentences with the correct form of the words in parentheses.*

1. The singers sang very _____badly_____ . I couldn't hear them _____ .
   (bad)   (good)

2. They sang too _____ . Their voices sounded _____ .
   (soft)   (weak)

3. Their costumes looked _____ , and they danced _____ .
   (beautiful)   (good)

4. We tried _____ to get _____ tickets.
   (hard)   (good)

5. Our seats were not _____ to the stage. It was _____ to see.
   (close)   (hard)

6. We arrived _____ , but the show started _____ .
   (early)   (late)

7. After the show, we left _____ . The traffic moved _____ .
   (quick)   (slow)

4 **EDIT** • *Read this journal entry. There are thirteen mistakes in the use of adjectives and adverbs. Find and correct them. The first mistake is already corrected.*

Last night I went to my first baseball game! I had a
           wonderful
~~wonderfully~~ time. We had great seats, and I could see very

good. Jon knows the game perfect, and he explained the

rules very clearly. Sometimes the game moves slow. Not much

happens. But then all at once it becomes exciting.

The other team's pitcher (the pitcher throws the ball) threw the ball hardly

and fast. One time the ball hit the batter (the batter usually hits *the ball*!). That

can be dangerous, because the ball is very hard and it moves very fastly. But it

didn't hurt him bad, and he could stay in the game. That was lucky for our

team. The next time he was at bat, he hit the ball hard and far. The ball flew

quick out of the field. That's called a "home run." The crowd stood up and

screamed loud. They were really happily. The final score was 10 to 3. Our team

won easy.

The game is just part of the event. In addition, we ate some typical "ball

park" food—hot dogs (a type of sausage) and French fries. It tasted greatly

with some cold soda.

The day was perfectly. I had a really great time, and I am looking forward

to the next game.

SelfTest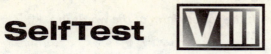

Circle the letter of the correct answer to complete each sentence.

EXAMPLE: Carlos _____ a student.   A B ⓒ D
    (A) are   (C) is
    (B) does   (D) were

1. The teacher seems _____.   A B C D
    (A) nice   (C) as nice as
    (B) nicely   (D) nicest

2. It was a _____ hot day.   A B C D
    (A) more   (C) enough
    (B) very   (D) most

3. My house isn't as old _____ yours.   A B C D
    (A) than   (C) as
    (B) like   (D) —

4. Lila is more athletic _____ her sister.   A B C D
    (A) as   (C) that
    (B) than   (D) —

5. She's fast, but he's faster _____.   A B C D
    (A) as   (C) enough
    (B) than   (D) —

6. That's the _____ car in the store!   A B C D
    (A) expensive   (C) most expensive
    (B) more expensive (D) too expensive

7. She sings _____.   A B C D
    (A) beautiful   (C) more beautiful
    (B) beautifully   (D) the most beautiful

8. My coffee isn't hot _____.   A B C D
    (A) very   (C) enough
    (B) too   (D) most

9. He works _____ and gets good grades.   A B C D
    (A) hard   (C) as hard as
    (B) hardly   (D) hard as

10. Alex is _____ student in his class.   A B C D
    (A) a best   (C) better
    (B) the best   (D) best

SECTION TWO

Each sentence has four underlined parts. The four underlined parts are marked A, B, C, and D.
Circle the letter of the part that is NOT CORRECT.

EXAMPLE:

Carla <u>is</u> a student, but she <u>are</u> <u>not</u> in school <u>today</u>.   A Ⓑ C D
     A   B   C   D

11. This book is a <u>good gift</u> because it has <u>most</u> <u>amazing</u>   A B C D
             A   B   C
    facts <u>in the world</u>.
           D

12. This <u>new bag</u> looks <u>very</u> <u>nice</u>, but it isn't <u>enough big</u> for me.   A B C D
        A   B   C   D

13. The <u>traffic</u> was <u>very</u> <u>bad</u>, so I arrived at school <u>lately</u>.   A B C D
       A   B C   D

14. The <u>coffee</u> wasn't <u>hot</u> <u>enough</u> and it tasted <u>terribly</u>.   A B C D
       A   B   C   D

15. Phoenix is <u>as hot as</u> Taipei, but it's not <u>as rainy</u> <u>as</u> or <u>as big</u>.   A B C D
          A   B   C   D

16. English wasn't <u>as</u> <u>easier</u> as Chinese for Aki, but it wasn't   A B C D
               A   B
    <u>too</u> <u>difficult</u>.
     C   D

17. This was <u>the worse</u> day of the week—it rained <u>hard</u>, and   A B C D
           A   B
    then it <u>got</u> <u>hot</u>.
          C D

18. Leyla is the <u>best</u> runner <u>in her class</u>, so she won the <u>race</u> <u>easy</u>.   A B C D
             A   B   C   D

19. She skated <u>well</u>, and she looked <u>beautifully</u>, but she didn't   A B C D
             A   B
    get a <u>perfect</u> <u>score</u>.
        C   D

20. <u>This</u> isn't the <u>most good</u> cake, but it's <u>good</u> and <u>cheap</u>.   A B C D
    A   B   C   D

21. It was <u>very</u> <u>cold</u>, but I wore a <u>heavily</u> coat and I felt <u>warm</u>.   A B C D
        A   B   C   D

22. Mario's has <u>the best</u> noodles in town, but Ben's is <u>cheapest</u>   A B C D
             A   B
    <u>than</u> Mario's and Pizza Oven is <u>closer</u>.
     C   D

23. Math is my <u>most bad</u> <u>subject</u>, so I'm studying <u>late</u> for the <u>big</u> test.   A B C D
           A   B   C   D

24. The <u>young</u> skaters practiced <u>hard</u>, and they never felt   A B C D
       A   B
    <u>nervously</u> in <u>big</u> competitions.
     C   D

25. The house is <u>big enough</u> for a <u>large family</u>, but it's <u>big too</u> for a   A B C D
             A   B   C
    <u>small one</u>.
     D

Ability: *Can, Could*

1. **AFFIRMATIVE AND NEGATIVE STATEMENTS; PRESENT AND PAST •** *Look at the chart. Complete the statements. Use contractions when possible.*

English Ability		
Student: Uta Schmidt		
	Last Year	**This Year**
Talk about daily activites	✔	✔
Talk on the phone		✔
Give a speech		
Write a letter	✔	✔
Write a report		✔
Read a book	✔	✔
Read the newspaper		✔
Understand a movie		✔
Understand the TV news		

1. Uta _____can talk_____ about daily activities this year. She _____could talk_____ about them last year too.

2. She _____ on the phone last year. She _____ on the phone now.

3. She _____ a speech in English last year. She still _____ a speech.

4. She _____ a letter now. She _____ one last year too.

5. She _____ a report last year. She _____ a report now.

6. She _____ a book in English now. She _____ a book last year.

7. She _____ the newspaper last year. She _____ it now.

8. She _____ a movie last year. She _____ a movie now.

9. She _____ the TV news last year. She still _____ it.

10. Uta _____ do many more things now than she _____ do last year!

2 **YES/NO QUESTIONS AND SHORT ANSWERS** • *Ask questions with the words in parentheses.*
Answer the questions.

1. **Q:** _Can Sadak speak English now?_
      (Sadak / speak English / now)
   A: _Yes, he can_ . He speaks it very well.

2. **Q:** _____
      (your brother / drive / last year)
   A: _____ . He just learned last month.

3. **Q:** _____
      (your sister / understand / the movie / last night)
   A: _____ . She understood it very well.

4. **Q:** _____
      (your mother / still / run fast)
   A: _____ . She runs faster than me!

5. **Q:** _____
      (she / swim / as a child)
   A: _____ . And she still _____ . She never learned to swim.

6. **Q:** _____
      (your brother / win a race / now)
   A: _____ . He doesn't run fast enough.

3 **WH- QUESTIONS** • *Ask questions about the underlined words.*

1. Marta can speak <u>three</u> languages. What about you?

   How many languages can you speak?

2. As a teenager, Deven could play tennis <u>for hours</u>. What about his sister?

   _____

3. In high school, Hak-Kun could jump <u>3 feet</u> high. What about his brother?

   _____

4. Malak can read <u>four</u> books a week. What about you?

   _____

5. As a child, Jarek could play <u>the piano and the violin</u>. What about Ana?

   _____

6. My brother can eat <u>a pint</u> of ice cream at one time. What about you?

   _____

7. Cruz could fall asleep <u>on a chair</u> as a child. What about your little sister?

   _____

UNIT 36

Suggestions:
Why don't, Let's, How about

---

1 **SUGGESTIONS WITH WHY DON'T** • *Complete these suggestions with* **Why don't** *or* **Why doesn't**.

1. **A:** I'm tired.

   B: ___Why don't you___ take a break?

2. **A:** My brother is unhappy with his apartment.

   B: _____ move?

3. **A:** I'm hungry.

   B: Me too. _____ get something to eat?

4. **A:** My parents and I are going to spend the summer in Italy.

   B: _____ call Emilia when you're there?

5. **A:** My sister wants to learn English.

   B: _____ take classes at our school?

6. **A:** My car is at the mechanic's.

   B: _____ give you a ride home? My car is right across the street.

7. **A:** Alex and Blaire love jazz.

   B: _____ get tickets to Friday's concert?

8. **A:** I'm going to be late.

   B: _____ take the train?

2 **SUGGESTIONS WITH LET'S: AFFIRMATIVE AND NEGATIVE** • *Complete these suggestions with* **Let's** *or* **Let's not** *and the verbs in parentheses.*

1. ___Let's get___ something to eat. I'm hungry.
   (get)

2. _____. I don't want to be late.
   (hurry)

3. _____ the bus. The train is faster.
   (take)

4. There's Pauline. _____ her to come with us. She's very nice.
   (ask)

5. _____ pizza again. Three times a week is too much!
   (have)

6. _____ to the library after lunch. I have to return some books.
   (go)

7. _____ too long. I want to get home before 5:00.
   (stay)

8. _____ TV tonight. There's a good movie on channel 4.
   (watch)

3 **SUGGESTIONS WITH HOW ABOUT** • *Complete these suggestions with **How about** and the correct form of the words from the box.*

get	invite	go	put
ride	talk	~~stay~~	study

1. ___How about staying___ home tonight? I'm tired.

2. I'm thirsty. _____ something to drink at the cafeteria?

3. _____ to the movies this weekend?

4. Next Friday is Ada's birthday. _____ her to dinner?

5. It's a nice day. _____ our bikes in the park?

6. We have a test on Friday. _____ for it together on Thursday?

7. Those are nice flowers. _____ them in this vase?

8. I know you're angry at Tom. _____ to him about the problem?

4 **SUGGESTIONS WITH WHY DON'T AND LET'S** • *Complete these conversations with **why don't**, **why doesn't**, **let's**, or **let's not** and the correct form of the verbs in parentheses.*

1. **A:** It's a nice day. ___Why don't we go___ for a walk in the park?
   (go)

   B: Good idea. _____ some sandwiches and take them with us.
   (make)

2. **A:** I'm having trouble in my math class.

   B: _____ Professor Schumacher for help?
   (ask)

3. **A:** _____ TV.
   (watch)

   B: OK. But _____ *The Real Thing*. I hate that show.
   (watch)

4. **A:** _____ dinner together?
   (make)

   B: OK. _____ some of our classmates.
   (invite)

5. **A:** My sister wants to meet more people. She doesn't have any friends here.

   B: _____ one of the school clubs?
   (join)

6. **A:** _____ dancing Saturday night.
   (go)

   B: Good idea. _____ that new dance club near school?
   (try)

7. **A:** _____ out tonight. I'm too tired.
   (go)

   B: OK. _____ home. We can watch TV or listen to music.
   (stay)

8. **A:** _____ the apartment. It's really messy.
   (clean)

   B: OK. _____ with the living room? It looks the worst.
   (start)

Requests:
Will, Would, Can, Could

1 **REQUESTS** • *Complete these requests with the words in parentheses.*

1. I'm having trouble with my homework. _____Could you help_____ me?
   (Could / help)

2. It's hot in here. _____ the window?
   (Can / open)

3. I don't understand this. _____ it to me?
   (Would / explain)

4. We're going to be late. _____?
   (Will / hurry)

5. This is heavy. _____ it for me?
   (Could / carry)

6. We need some more bread. _____ some on the way home?
   (Can / get)

7. _____ this book to Diana? She forgot to take it with her.
   (Would / give)

8. _____ me tomorrow?
   (Will / call)

2 **WORD ORDER WITH PLEASE** • *Unscramble these requests.*

1. _____Could you please mail this?_____
   (you • this • please • could • mail)

2. _____
   (call • please • will • me • you)

3. _____
   (you • can • please • me • help)

4. _____
   (be • would • please • you • quiet)

5. _____
   (door • could • the • please • you • close)

6. _____
   (please • wait • you • can)

7. _____
   (you • please • could • the • dishes • wash)

8. _____
   (you • please • early • would • come)

3 **SHORT ANSWERS** • *Read these requests. Circle the correct answers.*

1. **A:** Could you give me a ride home?
   B: Sure / Sorry, I can't. My car is at the mechanic's.

2. **A:** Would you please call me tomorrow night?
   B: Of course / Sorry, I can't. What time should I call?

3. A: Will you help me with my homework?

B: <u>No problem / Sorry, I can't</u>. I don't have time tonight.

4. A: Would you do the dishes tonight?

B: <u>Sure / Sorry, I can't</u>. I'll do them right after dinner.

5. A: Could you lend me some money until tomorrow?

B: <u>No problem / I can't</u>. How much do you need?

6. A: Can you explain this paragraph to me?

B: <u>Certainly / No, I can't</u>. I don't understand it.

4 **REQUESTS AND SHORT ANSWERS •** *Read the "to do" list. Complete the conversations with requests and shorts answers. There are several ways to complete the sentences.*

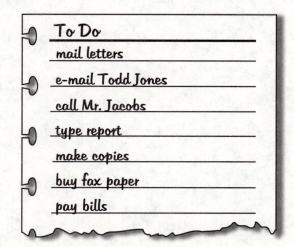

To Do
mail letters
e-mail Todd Jones
call Mr. Jacobs
type report
make copies
buy fax paper
pay bills

1. A: _Could you mail_ these letters?

B: _Sure_. I'll take them to the post office right now.

2. A: _____ Todd Jones about the meeting?

B: _____. What's his e-mail address?

3. A: _____ Mr. Jacobs? I need to change his appointment.

B: _____. I'll call right now.

4. A: _____ this report now?

B: _____. The computers aren't working now.

5. A: _____ of this article? I need ten copies.

B: _____. I'll do it before I leave for the day.

6. A: _____ fax paper? We don't have any left.

B: _____. How much should I get?

7. A: _____ these bills? They're due this week.

B: _____. I'll do it right now.

UNIT
38

Permission:
May, Can, Could

---

1 **QUESTIONS** • *Read these statements. Complete the questions.*

1. I'd like to park here.

May _____ I park here? _____

2. We'd like to swim in the lake.

Can _____

3. She'd like to use the phone.

Could _____

4. I'd like to take the test now.

May _____

5. Henri wants to borrow the car.

Can _____

6. I'd like to take your picture.

Could _____

7. I'd like to use my cell phone.

May _____

8. We'd like to leave now.

Could _____

2 **WORD ORDER WITH PLEASE** • *Unscramble these requests.*

1. _____ May I please use the phone? _____
(use • the • please • may • I • phone)

2. _____
(we • please • seats • our • can • change)

3. _____
(I • could • question • ask • a • please)

4. _____
(I • now • please • can • leave)

5. _____
(open • please • I • the • window • could)

6. _____
(sit • may • please • here • we)

3 **ANSWERS** • *Check the correct answers.*

1. **A:** Can we swim here?

    B: _____. Have fun! The water's great!

    ☑ Sure   ❏ No, please don't

2. **A:** Could I please open the window?

    B: _____. Go ahead.

    ❏ Yes, you can   ❏ Yes, you could

3. **A:** May I use my calculator during the test?

    B: _____. Sorry!

    ❏ Yes, you may   ❏ No, you may not

4. **A:** Can we park here?

    B: _____. It's a no-parking zone.

    ❏ Certainly   ❏ No, you can't

5. **A:** Could I please use the phone?

    B: _____. It's on the table near the door.

    ❏ Sure   ❏ No, please don't

4 **QUESTIONS AND ANSWERS** • *Complete the questions with the words in parentheses and answer them. There is sometimes more than one correct answer.*

A: This is our first time here. ___Can I ask___ you a few questions?
           1. (Can / ask)

B: ___Of course___. I'm happy to answer all your questions.
   2.

A: We're hungry. _____ to the dining room now?
         3. (Can / go)

B: _____. The dining room doesn't open until noon.
   4.

A: My cell phone isn't working. _____ yours?
          5. (May / use)

B: _____. Here it is.
   6.

A: I brought my radio. _____ to music?
          7. (Could / listen)

B: _____. But, please, not too loud.
   8.

A: _____ the swimming pool now?
  9. (May / use)

B: _____. There's no swimming at night. It's not safe.
   10.

A: _____ an extra key to our room?
 11. (Could / have)

B: _____. Here's another key.
   12.

SelfTest

SECTION ONE

Circle the letter of the correct answer to complete each sentence.

EXAMPLE: Carlos _____ a student.   A B Ⓒ D

    (A) are   (C) is

    (B) does   (D) were

1. Monique took lessons, and now she can _____ well.   A B C D
    (A) dance   (C) to dance
    (B) dances   (D) dancing

2. Chen couldn't _____ last year.   A B C D
    (A) drive   (C) drove
    (B) drives   (D) driving

3. How fast _____ run?   A B C D
    (A) you can   (C) you can't
    (B) can you   (D) can't you

4. Let's _____ now.   A B C D
    (A) leave   (C) leaving
    (B) leaves   (D) to leave

5. How about _____ for a drive?   A B C D
    (A) go   (C) going
    (B) goes   (D) to go

6. Why _____ she change jobs?   A B C D
    (A) don't   (C) no
    (B) doesn't   (D) not

7. Let's _____ home tonight.   A B C D
    (A) no stay   (C) isn't staying
    (B) don't stay   (D) not stay

8. —Could you call me tonight?   A B C D
    —_____ I'll call you at 7:00.
    (A) Yes, I could.   (C) No problem.
    (B) No, I couldn't.   (D) Yes, you can.

9. Can I _____ a question?   A B C D
    (A) ask   (C) to ask
    (B) asking   (D) —

10. —May we park here?   A B C D
    —No, you _____. The sign says NO PARKING.
    (A) mayn't   (C) don't
    (B) can't   (D) aren't

Each sentence or pair of sentences has four underlined parts. The four underlined parts are marked A, B, C, and D. Circle the letter of the part that is NOT CORRECT.

EXAMPLE:

Carla <u>is</u> a student, but she <u>are</u> <u>not</u> in school <u>today</u>.   A (B) C D
    A   B C   D

11. <u>Will</u> you <u>open please</u> the door, and <u>could</u> you <u>give</u> me those books   A B C D
    A   B   C   D
over there?

12. <u>Let's</u> you <u>invite</u> more people, so we <u>can</u> <u>have</u> two teams?   A B C D
    A   B   C   D

13. Kim's parents spoke Korean, so he <u>can</u> <u>speak</u> it, but he <u>can't</u>   A B C D
                                A   B   C
<u>reads</u> it.
 D

14. <u>Let's</u> <u>a party have</u> for Tina's birthday! Carla, <u>will</u> you <u>bake</u>   A B C D
    A   B   C   D
your famous chocolate cake?

15. <u>Sure</u>, but let's <u>don't</u> <u>invite</u> too many people. We <u>can't make</u>   A B C D
    A   B   C   D
a lot of noise.

16. Van <u>has</u> a big house, so <u>why</u> <u>we don't</u> have the party <u>there?</u>   A B C D
        A   B   C   D

17. <u>May please I</u> <u>leave</u> early? I <u>can stay</u> late <u>tomorrow</u>.   A B C D
    A   B   C   D

18. <u>Of course</u>. But I <u>can't</u> type, so <u>may you</u> <u>finish</u> the report first?   A B C D
    A   B   C   D

19. I can <u>play</u> the piano a little <u>now</u>, but I <u>can no</u> <u>play</u> perfectly.   A B C D
        A   B   C   D

20. You <u>can</u> <u>run</u> really fast! How fast <u>you could</u> run in high school<u>?</u>   A B C D
        A   B   C   D

21. <u>Would</u> you <u>lend please</u> me some money? I <u>can't</u> <u>find</u> my wallet.   A B C D
    A   B   C   D

22. <u>May</u> you <u>help</u> me with my bag<u>?</u> It's very heavy, and I   A B C D
    A   B   C
<u>can't carry</u> it.
 D

23. <u>You could</u> <u>turn</u> off the TV, <u>please</u>? Kathy's on the phone,   A B C D
    A   B   C
and I <u>can't hear</u>.
       D

24. Tania <u>can</u> <u>speak</u> English now, but she <u>can't</u> <u>speak</u> it when   A B C D
          A   B   C   D
she was a child.

25. I <u>can't swim</u> well, so <u>let's not</u> <u>swimming</u> so far out<u>.</u>   A B C D
      A   B   C   D

Desires:
Would like, Would rather

1   **STATEMENTS WITH WOULD LIKE** • *Write statements with* **would like**. *Use pronouns (***I, you, he, she, we, they***) and contractions.*

1. **Girl:** Can I have a piece of cake?

   She'd like a piece of cake.

2. **Man:** Let's go to the movies.

   _____

3. **Students:** Can we take a break?

   _____

4. **Woman:** Can I have a cup of coffee?

   _____

5. **You:** I want to finish this exercise.

   _____

6. **You and a classmate:** Can we leave now?

   _____

2   **STATEMENTS WITH WOULD RATHER** • *Complete the statements with* **would rather** *or* **would rather not** *and the words in parentheses. Use contractions.*

1. The cake looks good, but I _'d rather have_____ the pie.
                                         (have)

2. I _____ swimming. The water is too cold.
         (go)

3. She _____ the train. The bus is too slow.
            (take)

4. He _____ late. He wants to get home early.
          (stay)

5. I _____ online. The stores are too crowded.
        (shop)

6. We _____ a new car. It's too expensive.
         (buy)

7. She _____ an e-mail. She doesn't like to talk on the phone.
          (send)

8. I _____ out tonight. I'd like to stay home and read.
        (go)

9. The jacket is nice, but I _____ a sweater.
                        (wear)

10. He hurt his leg. He _____ today.
                  (run)

3 **QUESTIONS AND SHORT ANSWERS** • *Look at the survey. Complete the interview between* Travel Magazine (TM) *and* Steve Parker (SP). *Ask questions with the words in parentheses and answer them.*

Transportation Survey: Greece
Name: Steve Parker

Number the types of long-distance transportation from 1–5.   1 = your favorite

car	3
bus	5
train	2
boat	4
airplane	1

TM: Think about this: You're going to travel from Greece to Turkey.

How ___would you like to get___ there? _____?
     1. (like / get)   **2. (like / fly)**

SP: ___Yes, I would___ . The plane is my favorite way to travel.
        3.

TM: In Greece, you can travel by bus or train. _____ the bus?
                                          4. (rather / take)

SP: _____ .
        5.

TM: What about the train or car? _____ a car?
                            6. (rather / rent)

SP: _____ .
        7.

TM: And our last question. _____ by boat in Greece?
                      8. (like / travel)

SP: _____ . I get seasick!
        9.

4 **EDIT** • *Read this survey report. Find and correct six mistakes in the use of* **would like** *and* **would rather***. The first mistake is already corrected.*

Survey Report

Steve Parker completed the transportation survey and answered
some interview questions. According to Parker, for a business trip
he'd always like ^to^ fly. He'd not rather take the train or the bus. One of
the questions was: You would rather drive or take the train? He
rather drive. He really hates the bus. He'd rather not takes it. In fact,
he said, "I'd rather walking!"

Possibility:
May, Might, Could

1 **MEANING** • *Read these sentences. Check the correct column.*

	DEFINITELY	POSSIBLY
1. I'll call you tomorrow.	✔	
2. It might rain in the evening.		
3. He couldn't be right.		
4. They could be late.		
5. I may not take a vacation.		
6. We won't have the time.		
7. It's going to be difficult.		
8. We might not be home.		

2 **AFFIRMATIVE AND NEGATIVE STATEMENTS** • *Complete these sentences with the words in parentheses. Choose between affirmative and negative.*

1. Don't wait for me. I _____may not get_____ there on time.
   (may / get)

2. I _____ that coat. It's too expensive.
   (might / buy)

3. Take a sweater. It _____ colder later.
   (could / get)

4. I _____ to the movies tonight. Why don't you come too?
   (might / go)

5. It _____ tomorrow. It's going to be much too warm.
   (could / snow)

6. Hisae _____ you tomorrow. I gave her your number.
   (might / call)

7. Ari _____ to work. He's feeling sick.
   (might / go)

8. Rachel and Émile _____ to France. They miss their friends and family there.
   (may / return)

9. The bank _____ open tomorrow. It's a holiday.
   (might / be)

10. Carmen _____ her job. She's very unhappy with it.
    (might / leave)

11. My car _____ a problem. It's making a strange sound.
    (may / have)

12. I _____ to the party. I have too much work.
    (might / go)

3 **YES/NO QUESTIONS AND SHORT ANSWERS** • *Look at Dušan's "to do" list for tomorrow. He put a question mark (?) next to the activities he's not sure about. Ask and answer questions about his plans. Use* **be going** *to for the questions.*

1. **Q:** Is he going to go to the gym?

   A: He might not. . He hurt his leg last week.

2. **Q:** Is he going to go shopping for food?

   A: Yes, he is.

3. **Q:** _____

   A: _____ I think he's planning a party.

4. **Q:** _____

   A: _____

5. **Q:** _____

   A: _____ He talks to her a lot.

6. **Q:** _____

   A: _____

7. **Q:** _____

   A: _____

8. **Q:** _____

   A: _____ He's going to be really busy!

> *To Do*
> 1. go to gym?
> 2. go shopping for food
> 3. clean the living room?
> 4. bake a cake
> 5. call Lydia?
> 6. do English homework
> 7. e-mail Zlatan
> 8. do laundry?

4 **EDIT** • *Read this note. Find and correct five mistakes in the use of* **may**, **might**, *and* **could**. *The first mistake is already corrected.*

> Hi, Elissa—I'm going to go to the library, and I might ~~to~~ ^{not} be home
> before 6:00. I may to go to the supermarket on the way home. Do we
> need anything? Tania is going to come to dinner, but Anton mayn't. He
> doesn't feel well. May you make tacos for dinner? You know, it might be
> a good idea. It's easy, and everyone loves them. Oh, and please
> remember to close the window. It might rains. Call me. I have my cell
> with me. —Vania

Advice: *Should, Ought to*

1 **AFFIRMATIVE AND NEGATIVE STATEMENTS WITH SHOULD** • *Complete these statements with* **should** *or* **shouldn't** *and the correct verb from the box.*

ask	be	do	eat
go	~~study~~	wait	work

1. We have a test next week. We ___should study___ for it now. It's never too soon!

2. We _____ until the night before the test.

3. Jan doesn't understand something. She _____ the teacher to explain it.

4. Other students can help you too. You _____ in groups.

5. The night before the test, you _____ to bed late. Sleep is important.

6. You _____ breakfast the morning of the test. Food is important too.

7. You _____ nervous. Study hard, and you'll do well on the test!

8. After the test, you _____ something fun. Enjoy!

2 **SHOULD AND OUGHT TO: STATEMENTS** • *Rewrite the imperative sentences with* **should**, **shouldn't**, *or* **ought to.**

1. Visit Portugal. It's a very beautiful country. (should)
   You should visit Portugal.

2. Learn some Portuguese before your trip. (ought to)
   _____

3. Spend some time in Lisbon. (ought to)
   _____

4. Wear comfortable shoes. Lisbon has a lot of hills. (should)
   _____

5. Don't forget to take a dictionary! (should)
   _____

6. Try the seafood. It's delicious. (ought to)
   _____

7. Don't visit only Lisbon. Small towns are beautiful too. (should)
   _____

3 YES/NO QUESTIONS AND SHORT ANSWERS • *Complete these questions with the words in parentheses and short answers.*

1. **Q:** ___Should___ I ___rent___ a car?
   (rent)
   A: _____. It's the best way to see the country.

2. **Q:** _____ I _____ in August?
   (go)
   A: _____. It's better to go in the spring or fall.

3. **Q:** I don't speak Portuguese. _____ I _____ Spanish there?
   (speak)
   A: _____. People in Portugal speak more English than Spanish.

4. **Q:** _____ I _____ the town of Marvao?
   (visit)
   A: _____. It's a very interesting place.

5. **Q:** _____ we _____ hotel reservations?
   (make)
   A: _____! Reserve before you go. It's a popular country.

6. **Q:** _____ I _____ you a postcard?
   (send)
   A: _____. I love to get postcards!

4 WH- QUESTIONS • *Read the answers and then ask questions about the underlined words.*

1. **A:** What should I eat in Portugal?
   B: You should eat <u>fish</u> in Portugal.

2. **A:** _____
   B: You should go <u>in the fall</u>.

3. **A:** _____
   B: You should go <u>to the southern coast</u>.

4. **A:** _____
   B: You should go there <u>by car</u>.

5. **A:** _____
   B: You should go there <u>because the beaches are beautiful</u>.

6. **A:** _____
   B: You should go for <u>two weeks or more</u>.

7. **A:** _____
   B: You should buy <u>a vase</u>. They make beautiful pottery.

Necessity: *Have to, Must, Don't have to, Must not*

1 **AFFIRMATIVE AND NEGATIVE STATEMENTS WITH HAVE TO** • *Look at Marta's and Anton's "to do" lists. Complete the statements with* **have to, don't have to, has to,** *or* **doesn't have to**.

Marta	*Anton*
do homework	*do homework*
study for test	*buy notebook*
research English paper	*write English paper*
read newspaper	*read newspaper*

1. Marta and Anton _____*have to*_____ do homework.

2. Marta _____ study for a test.

3. Anton _____ study for a test.

4. Marta _____ buy a notebook.

5. Anton _____ buy a notebook.

6. Anton _____ research an English paper.

7. Marta _____ research an English paper.

8. Marta _____ write an English paper.

9. Anton _____ write an English paper.

10. Marta and Anton _____ read the newspaper.

11. Marta and Anton _____ finish reading *Romeo and Juliet.*

What about you? Complete these sentences with your own information.

12. I _____ study for a test.

13. I _____ finish these exercises.

2 **QUESTIONS WITH HAVE TO** • *Complete these questions with the correct form of* **have to** *and the verbs in parentheses.*

1. _____*Do*_____ you ___*have to study*___ tonight?
   (study)

2. Why _____ she _____ a calculator?
   (use)

3. _____ your sister _____ a school uniform?
   (wear)

4. _____ your classmates _____ English in class?
   (speak)

5. _____ we _____ before 9:00?
       (arrive)

6. _____ Albert _____ a report?
                          (write)

7. When _____ he _____ his report?
                              (finish)

8. _____ we _____ now?
                    (leave)

3 **AFFIRMATIVE AND NEGATIVE STATEMENTS WITH MUST** • *Complete these school rules with* **must** *or* **must not**.

1. Students _____must_____ arrive on time.

2. They _____ be late.

3. Students _____ have a photo ID.

4. Students _____ run in the halls.

5. Students _____ chew gum in class.

6. They _____ bring a doctor's note for more than ten days of missed classes.

7. Students _____ wear clean clothes.

8. All students _____ follow these rules!

4 **DON'T HAVE TO *OR* MUST NOT** • *Complete these statements with* **don't have to**, **doesn't have to**, *or* **must not**.

1. Boys ___don't have to___ wear a tie to school.

2. Girls _____ wear skirts. Pants are fine.

3. Boys and girls _____ wear shorts. Long pants only.

4. You _____ smoke in school or in the school yard. It's against the rules.

5. Students _____ use calculators during a math test. Paper and pencil only!

6. Students _____ use their cell phones in class or in the school library. Your classmates need a quiet place to learn and study.

7. Students _____ bring their own computers. Each student will get one from the school.

8. Students _____ come to class late. Class starts at 9:00. Be there!

SelfTest

SECTION ONE

Circle the letter of the correct answer to complete each sentence.

EXAMPLE: Carlos _____ a student.   **A B ⒸD**

    (A) are   (C) is
    (B) does   (D) were

---

1. She would _____ a cup of coffee.   **A B C D**
   (A) like   (C) liking
   (B) likes   (D) to like

2. _____ you like a piece of cake now?   **A B C D**
   (A) Do   (C) Would
   (B) Are   (D) Could

3. He'd rather _____ .   **A B C D**
   (A) tea   (C) having tea
   (B) have tea   (D) has tea

4. My sister _____ rather live in the country.   **A B C D**
   (A) had   (C) did
   (B) would   (D) does

5. —Would you like soda?   **A B C D**
—_____ .
   (A) No, I don't   (C) Yes, please
   (B) Yes, I do   (D) I love soda

6. Take your umbrella. It _____ rain.   **A B C D**
   (A) might   (C) has to
   (B) might not (D) doesn't have to

7. Hugo might _____ you later.   **A B C D**
   (A) call   (C) calling
   (B) calls   (D) to call

8. She didn't study enough, so she _____ pass the test.   **A B C D**
   (A) may   (C) mightn't
   (B) may not   (D) may no

9. —_____ you be home tonight?   **A B C D**
—I may. I'm not sure.
   (A) May   (C) Will
   (B) Could   (D) Can

10. When _____ call you?
    (A) I should   (C) ought I
    (B) should I   (D) I ought to

A B C D

11. You don't like your job. Maybe you _____ get a new one.
    (A) would   (C) shouldn't
    (B) ought   (D) should

A B C D

12. Karl _____ to go on a business trip.
    (A) has   (C) must
    (B) have   (D) must no

A B C D

13. Students _____ chew gum. It's against the school rules.
    (A) have to   (C) don't have to
    (B) must   (D) must not

A B C D

SECTION TWO

Each sentence or pair of sentences has four underlined parts. The four underlined parts are marked A, B, C, and D. Circle the letter of the part that is NOT CORRECT.

EXAMPLE:

Carla is a student, but she are not in school today.
    A   B C   D

A (B) C D

14. I like coffee, but I'd rather to have tea tonight.
    A B   C   D

A B C D

15. Would you like staying home, or would you rather go out?
    A   B   C   D

A B C D

16. We'd like to get another car, but we'd not rather buy a new one.
    A   B   C   D

A B C D

17. Sonia might takes the train, or she might fly.
    A   B   C   D

A B C D

18. You really ought call your mother. You shouldn't worry her.
    A   B   C   D

A B C D

19. You must not wear a tie, but you ought to wear a jacket.
    A   B   C   D

A B C D

20. Ana have to work tonight, but she doesn't have to work now.
    A   B   C   D

A B C D

21. Do you want to leave now, or would you rather to stay?
    A   B   C   D

A B C D

22. It may rain tomorrow, but it might not snow. It's much too warm.
    A B   C   D

A B C D

23. Should we take the bus, or we should drive?
    A   B   C   D

A B C D

24. You don't have to go to the party, but you should to send a gift.
    A   B   C   D

A B C D

25. I should buy the cheaper camera, but I rather get this one.
    A   B   C   D

A B C D

UNIT 43

Gerunds and Infinitives

1 **FORM** • *Complete with the correct gerunds and infinitives.*

BASE FORM	GERUND	INFINITIVE
1. go	*going*	*to go*
2. write	_____	_____
3. swim	_____	_____
4. walk	_____	_____
5. hurry	_____	_____
6. hit	_____	_____
7. move	_____	_____
8. exercise	_____	_____

2 **AFFIRMATIVE STATEMENTS** • *Complete these statements with the gerund or infinitive form of the verbs in parentheses.*

1. We want _____*to go*_____ to the beach tomorrow.
       (go)

2. I really enjoy _____ in the ocean.
          (swim)

3. We plan _____ early in the morning.
        (leave)

4. I'd like _____ all day.
        (stay)

5. My brother always avoids _____ in the sun too long.
              (be)

6. I suggested _____ a beach umbrella.
            (bring)

7. He needs _____ careful.
           (be)

8. I promised _____ sandwiches.
            (make)

9. My brother suggested _____ soda at the beach.
                 (buy)

10. I feel like _____ some friends.
            (invite)

11. I asked my brother _____ us.
               (drive)

12. I can't wait _____!
           (go)

3 **NEGATIVE STATEMENTS** • *Complete these statements with the gerund or infinitive form of the verbs in parentheses.*

1. My cousin decided _____not to go_____ with us.
   (not go)

2. My brother considered _____.
   (not drive)

3. We agreed _____ all day.
   (not stay)

4. I planned _____ before 4:00.
   (not leave)

5. We discussed _____ dinner there.
   (not have)

6. My brother recommended _____ too many people.
   (not invite)

7. I promised _____ in the sun all the time.
   (not stay)

8. My friend suggested _____ out too far.
   (not swim)

4 **AFFIRMATIVE OR NEGATIVE STATEMENTS** • *Read each statement or question. Then complete the summary. Use gerunds and infinitives. Choose between affirmative and negative.*

1. **WOLFGANG:** I'll get some soda.

   (summary) Wolfgang offered _____to get some soda._____

2. **MARIE:** Can I have a sandwich?

   (summary) Marie wanted _____

3. **WOLFGANG:** The water is rough. Don't go too far.

   (summary) Wolfgang suggested _____

4. **MARIE:** Don't worry. I won't go far.

   (summary) Marie promised _____

5. **WOLFGANG:** I'm tired. I'm going to read.

   (summary) Wolfgang feels like _____

6. **MARIE:** Let's get some ice cream.

   (summary) Marie suggested _____

7. **WOLFGANG:** I don't eat ice cream. I stopped.

   (summary) Wolfgang quit _____

8. **MARIE:** It's getting late. Let's leave now.

   (summary) Marie would like _____

Infinitives of Purpose

1   **AFFIRMATIVE STATEMENTS** • *Answer the questions with the correct words from the box and the infinitive of purpose.*

make spaghetti sauce	buy some eggs	learn Spanish
make an appointment	mail a package	study for a test

1. Why did you go to the post office?

   I went to the post office to mail a package.

2. Why did she go to the supermarket?

   _____

3. Why did he call Dr. Ellin?

   _____

4. Why did they go to the library?

   _____

5. Why did she go to Mexico?

   _____

6. Why did they need a lot of tomatoes?

   _____

2   **NEGATIVE STATEMENTS** • *Rewrite these sentences. Use **in order not to**.*

1. I ran to class because I didn't want to be late.

   I ran to class in order not to be late.

2. She made a shopping list because she didn't want to forget things.

   _____

3. He eats only low-fat food because he doesn't want to gain weight.

   _____

4. They spoke softly because they didn't want to wake the baby.

   _____

5. She copies all her files onto CDs because she doesn't want to lose important information.

   _____

3 **AFFIRMATIVE AND NEGATIVE STATEMENTS •** *Complete these conversations with the infinitive form of the correct verb from the boxes.*

keep	practice	ask	meet	spend	~~stay~~

1. **A:** Why do you drink so much coffee?

   B: _____To stay_____ awake.

2. **A:** Why does Jason spend so much time at the Internet Café?

   B: He goes there _____ people.

3. **A:** You and Alicia rent a lot of Spanish videos. Why is that?

   B: We watch them _____ our Spanish.

4. **A:** When I go shopping, I only take $50 with me _____ too much money.

   B: Good idea! I have to try that!

5. **A:** The movie theater is always really cold.

   B: I know. I always bring a sweater _____ warm.

6. **A:** Why did Antonio call?

   B: _____ a question about the homework.

buy	do	invite	study	miss	remind

7. **A:** Why does Sara always leave the office before 5:00?

   B: She has to leave early _____ the 5:10 bus.

8. **A:** I saw you at the library yesterday.

   B: I went there _____ my history homework.

9. **A:** Why do you call Jan every day?

   B: _____ her to water the plants. She often forgets.

10. **A:** I saw you at the post office this morning.

    B: I went there _____ stamps.

11. **A:** Why did you call Anton?

    B: _____ him to my party. It's next Friday night.

12. **A:** Why did you go to France?

    B: _____ French. I love the language.

SelfTest

Circle the letter of the correct answer to complete each sentence.

EXAMPLE: Carlos _____ a student.	A B Ⓒ D
(A) are (C) is	
(B) does (D) were	

1. Vadim enjoys _____ TV.   **A B C D**
   (A) watch   (C) watches
   (B) to watch   (D) watching

2. Ryoko promised _____ late.   **A B C D**
   (A) not be   (C) being not
   (B) not to be   (D) not being

3. We avoided _____ on that road.   **A B C D**
   (A) drive   (C) driving
   (B) to drive   (D) drove

4. —Why did you leave so early?   **A B C D**
   —_____ there on time.
   (A) For getting   (C) Get
   (B) Getting   (D) To get

5. Do you want _____ here?   **A B C D**
   (A) to stop   (C) stopping
   (B) stop   (D) we stop

6. They regret _____ to the party.   **A B C D**
   (A) no going   (C) not going
   (B) not to go   (D) going not

7. We went there _____ some friends.   **A B C D**
   (A) meet   (C) to meet
   (B) met   (D) meeting

8. She wears a watch _____ not to be late.   **A B C D**
   (A) for   (C) to
   (B) in order   (D) in

9. —_____ did you call Sonia?   **A B C D**
   —To get the homework.
   (A) Who   (C) How
   (B) What   (D) Why

10. They called _____ my appointment.   **A B C D**
    (A) me to change   (C) to change me
    (B) to me change   (D) for changing

11. I recommended _____ that movie.   A B C D
     (A) see   (C) seeing
     (B) to see   (D) saw

12. We plan _____ it again   A B C D
     (A) rent   (C) renting
     (B) to rent   (D) we'll rent

13. They _____ getting a new car.   A B C D
     (A) agreed   (C) decided
     (B) chose   (D) discussed

SECTION TWO

*Each sentence has four underlined parts. The four underlined parts are marked
A, B, C, and D. Circle the letter of the part that is NOT CORRECT.*

EXAMPLE:

Carla <u>is</u> a student, but she <u>are</u> <u>not</u> in school <u>today</u>.   A (B) C D
    A   B   C   D

14. We decided <u>not</u> <u>to go</u> out because we <u>enjoy</u> <u>to stay</u> home.   A B C D
                 A   B   C   D

15. Todd suggested <u>taking</u> the train <u>in</u> order <u>not</u> <u>being</u> late.   A B C D
                     A   B   C   D

16. The doctor <u>recommended</u> <u>losing</u> weight, so I <u>quit</u> <u>to eat</u> desserts.   A B C D
                A   B   C   D

17. I needed <u>to go</u> to the library <u>for</u> <u>borrow</u> some books.   A B C D
             A B   C   D

18. She <u>agreed</u> <u>to buy</u> a used car in order <u>to not</u> <u>spend</u> too much   A B C D
         A   B   C   D
     money.

19. Marta <u>keeps</u> <u>practicing</u> her English <u>in order</u> not <u>forget</u> it.   A B C D
           A   B   C   D

20. Did you <u>finish</u> <u>writing</u> that report, or do you <u>need</u> more time   A B C D
             A   B   C
     <u>for finishing</u> it?
      D

21. I <u>expect</u> <u>to finish</u> it tomorrow, but I <u>want</u> <u>to checking</u> it before   A B C D
       A   B   C   D
     I send it.

22. We <u>discussed</u> <u>to buy</u> a new house, but then <u>chose</u> <u>not to</u> move.   A B C D
        A   B   C   D

23. Do you need <u>using</u> an alarm clock <u>in order</u> <u>not to</u> <u>sleep</u> too   A B C D
                 A   B   C   D
     late in the morning?

24. Cindi <u>hoped</u> <u>to stay</u> at her job, but they refused <u>giving</u> her   A B C D
           A   B   C
     more money, and she decided <u>to leave</u>.
                                  D

25. They <u>dislike</u> <u>not getting</u> exercise, so they decided <u>to walk</u> and   A B C D
          A   B   C
     <u>not taking</u> the bus.
      D

UNIT 45 **Prepositions** of Time

1 **MEANING • Circle the correct words to complete these conversations.**

1. **A:** (When) / How long do you get up?

   B: I always get up <u>at / on</u> 6:00.

2. **A:** <u>When / How long</u> did you stay at the party?

   B: We stayed <u>at / until</u> 10:00.

3. **A:** The train leaves <u>at / until</u> 7:00.

   B: But we have to get to the station <u>by / from</u> 6:45 to get a seat.

4. **A:** <u>When / How long</u> did you study for your math test?

   B: <u>During / For</u> three hours.

5. **A:** We're going to be in Rio <u>on / from</u> Monday <u>in / to</u> Wednesday.

   B: Good. I'll see you there <u>on / to</u> Wednesday.

6. **A:** Where are you going to be <u>at / during</u> the summer?

   B: We're going to be in Singapore <u>on / in</u> June and Australia <u>for / by</u> the rest of the summer.

7. **A:** Can I talk to you <u>during / on</u> the break?

   B: Sure. I'll be free <u>at / in</u> 12:00.

8. **A:** Hurry! The train leaves <u>by / in</u> a few minutes.

   B: Don't worry. I'l be there <u>by / in</u> 2:05.

9. **A:** Will Rob be home <u>at / in</u> 10:00 tonight?

   B: No. He works <u>at / in</u> night. He doesn't get home <u>in / until</u> midnight.

10. **A:** Mom and Dad flew on the Concorde <u>in / at</u> 1962.

    B: They told me about that. They were in Paris <u>in / for</u> a month.

2 **MEANING • Complete these sentences with the correct prepositions from the boxes. More than one answer is sometimes possible.**

after	at	during	in	~~on~~

1. _____On_____ Friday I flew to Bogotá.

2. It was my second trip _____ May.

3. _____ the flight I stayed in my seat and read a book.

112

4. We had lunch _____ 1:00.

5. _____ 1:30 they showed a movie.

at	for	in	on	until

6. We stayed in Bogotá _____ a week.

7. We stayed at a hotel _____ Monday.

8. _____ Monday we visited our friends and stayed with them.

9. _____ night we often went dancing.

10. I want to go back to Bogotá _____ the summer.

3 | **MEANING** • *Look at the calendar. Complete the sentences with the correct prepositions of time.*

DAILY PLANNER

Friday, Oct. 3, 2003

7:00 A.M.	*get up*	12:00 P.M.	*lunch (do Spanish homework)*
8:00 A.M.	*run 30 minutes*	1:00 P.M.	*art*
9:00 A.M.		2:00 P.M.	
10:00 A.M.	*Spanish*	3:00 P.M.	*catch 3:35 bus*
11:00 A.M.		4:00 P.M.	*arrive home*

1. This calendar page shows a student's activities ___*on*___ October 3, 2003.

2. Jennifer got up _____ 7:00 A.M.

3. She ran _____ school.

4. She ran _____ 8:30.

5. She was in her Spanish class _____ 9:00 _____ 11:00.

6. She had Spanish _____ two hours.

7. She had lunch _____ her Spanish class.

8. She ate _____ 12:00.

9. _____ lunch, she did her Spanish homework.

10. Her art class was _____ 1:00 _____ 2:00.

11. The bus left _____ 3:35.

12. She arrived home _____ 25 minutes.

UNIT 46 Prepositions of Place

1 **MEANING** • *Circle the correct words to complete these sentences.*

1. Bruno lives (in) / at Brazil.

2. He works <u>at</u> / <u>on</u> a small advertising company.

3. His office is <u>in</u> / <u>at</u> a building <u>across from</u> / <u>between</u> the post office.

4. Bruno doesn't live <u>near</u> / <u>far from</u> his office. He has to take the train.

5. He always does work <u>at</u> / <u>on</u> the train.

6. He eats lunch <u>in</u> / <u>on</u> a restaurant <u>next to</u> / <u>across</u> his office.

7. It's the only restaurant <u>in</u> / <u>on</u> the street.

8. I met Bruno <u>in</u> / <u>at</u> a party last year.

9. The party was <u>in</u> / <u>at</u> Rio de Janeiro.

10. It was <u>in</u> / <u>on</u> a very nice restaurant.

11. There were beautiful flowers <u>in</u> / <u>on</u> every table.

12. I sat <u>between</u> / <u>far</u> my boss and <u>he</u> / <u>him</u>.

2 **MEANING** • *Complete these conversations with the correct prepositions from the boxes. More than one answer is sometimes possible.*

in	~~near~~	on	on	between	over	under

1. **A:** Do you walk to school?

   B: Yes. My apartment is _____*near*_____ the school.

2. **A:** Where are your shoes?

   B: They're _____ the floor, _____ the bed.

3. **A:** I can't find my glasses.

   B: Look _____ the mirror! They're _____ your head!

4. **A:** Where should I hang this picture?

   B: Hang it _____ the couch.

5. **A:** Where's the café?

   B: It's _____ the bank and the post office.

at	in back of	next to	on	on

6. **A:** Where's the nearest music store?

   B: There's one _____ the library _____ Walker Street.

   It's _____ the right.

7. **A:** Where can I park my car?

   B: Park _____ the library. You can't see it from the street, but there's

   a parking lot there.

8. **A:** Do you know the exact address of the library?

   B: Yes. It's _____ 39 Walker Street.

3   **MEANING** • *Look at the picture. Complete the sentences with the correct prepositions of place. More than one answer is sometimes possible.*

1. This is a picture of the kitchen _____ in _____
   Jane's house.

2. Jane lives _____ England.

3. Her house is _____ Arthur Road.

4. It's _____ 2654 Arthur Road.

5. The sink is _____ the stove and the
   refrigerator.

6. There's a window _____ the sink.

7. The stove is _____ of the sink.

8. There's a pot _____ the stove.

9. There's a calendar _____ the wall.

10. The refrigerator is _____ of the sink.

11. There are a few bottles of soda _____
    the refrigerator.

12. There's a loaf of bread _____ the refrigerator.

2654 Arthur Road, England

13. There's a table _____ the kitchen.

14. There's a light. It's hanging _____ the table.

15. It's _____ the middle of the room.

16. There's a vase of flowers _____ the table.

17. There's a rug _____ the table.

18. The kitchen door is open. You can see the living room. It's _____ the kitchen.

UNIT 47   **Prepositions** of Movement

MEANING • *Look at the map. Circle the correct words to complete the paragraph.*

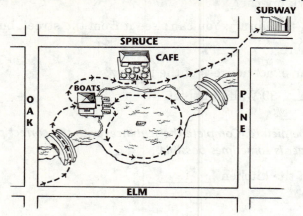

Yesterday we took a walk (to)/ toward the park. We walked along / through the park
         1.   **2.**

from / past Elm Street around / to Spruce Street. We began at the corner of Oak and Elm
 3.   **4.**

and walked along / around a path toward / across the lake. We walked across / past a small
          5.   **6.**   **7.**

bridge and continued to / in the lake. At the lake, we rented a small row boat. We got
                8.

on / into the boat and rowed around / through the lake. Then we got off / out of the boat
 9.   **10.**   **11.**

and went to / around the café. We sat there for an hour. We left the park and went
        12.

down / up the stairs to the subway station. Then we went home / to home by / with subway.
 13.   **14.**   **15.**

2 **MEANING •** *Complete these sentences with the correct prepositions from the boxes.*

by	in	~~out of~~	on	over

1. We got ___out of___ the taxi at the airport.
2. We like to travel _____ plane.
3. We got _____ the plane at 12:15.
4. We flew _____ the Atlantic Ocean.
5. We landed _____ Budapest.

116

along	into	through	toward	out of

6. We enjoyed walking _____ the river and watching the boats.

7. We saw an interesting building in the distance, and we walked _____ it.

8. We went _____ the building. It was a museum.

9. We walked _____ the museum for two hours and saw a lot of exhibits.

10. Then we walked _____ the museum and went back to our hotel.

down	off	on	under	up	through

11. The next morning, we left our hotel and got _____ the subway.

12. The subway travels _____ the streets.

13. You have to walk _____ steps to get to the train.

14. An agent sometimes walks _____ the train to check the passengers' tickets.

15. We reached our station, got _____ the train, and walked _____ the steps to the street.

3 **EDIT** • *Read this postcard. Find and correct seven mistakes in the use of prepositions of movement. The first mistake is already corrected.*

Hi, Ian!

    This city is great. Today we went for a long walk along ~~through~~ the beautiful river. Then we walked above this big hill. From the top of the hill we could look under the red rooftops of the city's old buildings. What a beautiful view! We were tired, so we walked out of a café and sat down for a cup of coffee. And that's where I am now. I'm writing postcards, and the server just put some little cakes in the table. They look delicious. After I eat them, I'm going to take the postcards toward the post office and mail them there. Then we'll go back to the hotel. Tomorrow is our last day. I had a great time, but I'm happy to go to home.

               See you soon. — M.

Ian Harlow
salita Montebello 8
16126 Genova
Italia

Two-Word Verbs:
Inseparable

---

1 **MEANING •** *Match each two-word verb with its meaning.*

TWO-WORD VERB

_i_	**1.** eat out
_____	**2.** get along
_____	**3.** hang up
_____	**4.** show up
_____	**5.** run into
_____	**6.** break down
_____	**7.** grow up
_____	**8.** go back
_____	**9.** keep on
_____	**10.** work out

MEANING

a. end a phone conversation

b. exercise

c. return

d. stop working

e. become an adult

f. continue

g. have a good relationship

h. meet by accident

i. eat in a restaurant

j. appear

2 **PREPOSITIONS •** *Circle the correct prepositions.*

1. Sonia went in / out with Paulo last night.

2. Her best friend went along / on with them.

3. They ended up / out at Joe's pizza place.

4. Some of their classmates turned down / up at Joe's.

5. They ran into / out their teacher there too.

6. They all hung out / up together for a few hours.

7. They got along / out really well.

8. Sonia wants to keep off / on seeing Paulo.

9. The three friends stayed over / up late talking.

10. Sonia didn't get back / up home until after 11:00.

11. They're going to get up / together again next week.

12. Sonia enjoys going out / up in a group.

13. She felt a little tired. She usually doesn't stay down / up late.

14. When she got home, she lay up / down on the couch and fell asleep.

15. The alarm clock rang at 7:00 A.M., and she got out / up.

3 **MEANING** • *Rewrite these sentences with the correct form of the two-word verbs in the box.*

break down	come about	come back	dress up
drop out	~~eat out~~	keep on	hang up
hang out	sign up	sit down	stay up

1. We <u>ate in a restaurant</u> last night.
   We ate out last night.

2. When did your TV <u>stop working</u>?
   _____

3. The students sometimes <u>spend time</u> together at the pizza place.
   _____

4. Sometimes it's difficult for Paulo to <u>remain awake</u> late.
   _____

5. Please don't <u>end this conversation</u> now.
   _____

6. <u>Take a seat</u> and relax.
   _____

7. How did that <u>happen</u>?
   _____

8. When will you <u>return</u>?
   _____

9. Sonia <u>put on special clothes</u> for her party.
   _____

10. They <u>continued</u> working until 6:00.
    _____

11. Mike was bored at school, so he <u>quit</u>.
    _____

12. I want to <u>register</u> for another language class.
    _____

Two-Word Verbs:
Separable

1 **MEANING** • *Match each two-word verb with its meaning.*

TWO-WORD VERB	MEANING
__h__ **1.** pick up	**a.** return something
_____ **2.** turn on	**b.** stop a machine
_____ **3.** look over	**c.** decrease the volume
_____ **4.** take back	**d.** give work to a teacher
_____ **5.** give up	**e.** put in the trash
_____ **6.** turn down	**f.** start a machine
_____ **7.** throw away	**g.** quit
_____ **8.** pick out	**h.** lift
_____ **9.** hand in	**i.** examine
_____ **10.** turn off	**j.** choose

2 **PREPOSITIONS** • *Circle the correct prepositions.*

1. Could you please hang on /(up) your coat in the closet?

2. Thanks for lending me the money. I'll pay you <u>back / up</u> tomorrow.

3. It's cold out. Put <u>on / up</u> your jacket.

4. The meeting is tomorrow at 3:00. Write it <u>down / in</u> or you'll forget.

5. Jason keeps calling me <u>down / up</u> and leaving messages on my answering machine.

6. The milk is bad. I'm going to take it <u>back / over</u> to the store.

7. Is the music too loud? I can turn it <u>down / up</u>.

8. Our neighbors asked us <u>out / over</u> for dinner at their house.

3 **SEPARABLE TWO-WORD VERBS AND PRONOUNS** • *Read these conversations. Complete them with the correct form of the two-word verbs. Use pronouns.*

1. A: Did you put away your books?

   B: No, but I'll ___put them away___ now.

2. A: Could you call Mr. Rivera up?

   B: I _____ yesterday.

3. A: Why did they put the meeting off?

   B: They _____ because of the storm.

4. A: When are you going to hand your report in?

   B: I _____ yesterday.

5. A: Could you please turn the TV down? I'm trying to study.

   B: No problem. I'll _____.

6. A: I'd like to ask Andrea over for dinner.

   B: Good idea. Let's _____ tonight.

7. A: You should do your report over. There are a lot of mistakes in it.

   B: OK. I'll _____.

8. A: I think we need to talk these problems over.

   B: You're right. Let's _____ at the meeting.

4 **MEANING •** *Rewrite these sentences with the correct form of the two-word verbs in the box. Sometimes there are two ways to write them. Write them both ways when possible.*

ask over	fill out	give back	~~hand in~~
look over	pick out	turn down	work out

1. I <u>gave my homework to my teacher</u>.

   I handed my homework in. OR I handed in my homework.

2. The problem was difficult. We <u>solved</u> it together.

   _____

3. The music is too loud. Please <u>decrease the volume</u>.

   _____

4. Ana is in town. Let's <u>invite</u> her for dinner.

   _____

5. Please <u>complete</u> this form with a pen.

   _____

6. Thanks for the pen. I'll <u>return</u> it after class.

   _____

7. I always <u>examine</u> my homework carefully before class.

   _____

8. There are a lot of nice shirts on sale. <u>Choose</u> the one you like best.

   _____

UNIT 50

Sentence Connectors:
and, but, or, so, because

1   *MEANING • Circle the correct words.*

1. I like to read, and / **but** I don't have much time.
2. Do you want to stay home, and / or do you want to go to the movies?
3. Neng-Tze was tired, but / so she went to bed early.
4. Carlos speaks English, and / but he speaks Spanish.
5. We're going to Brazil because / so we have family there.
6. It's cold out, and / so take your jacket.
7. I invited Alina to the party, so / but she can't come.
8. It's a nice day, so / but we're going to the beach.
9. I read the book, but / or I didn't understand the story.
10. And / Because I don't understand the story, I'll ask my teacher about it.

2   *MEANING AND PUNCTUATION • Complete these sentences with **because** or **so**. Add commas where necessary.*

1. Our computer is old ,so we're going to buy a new one.
2. We're buying a used car _____ a new one is too expensive.
3. _____ it was raining, they decided to stay home and watch TV.
4. It's 5:00 _____ we're going to stop working now.
5. She's studying hard _____ she has a test tomorrow.
6. He wants to lose weight _____ he's exercising a lot.
7. I'm calling Dara _____ I want to invite her to the party.
8. She's going to the supermarket _____ she needs potatoes.
9. I'm sending her a card _____ Friday is her birthday.
10. He loves comic books _____ he collects them.

3   *MEANING AND PUNCTUATION • Connect the two sentences with the words in parentheses. Decide on the correct order. Add commas where necessary.*

1. I'm going to take my umbrella. It's raining. (so)

   It's raining, so I'm going to take my umbrella.

2. I'm late. I have to hurry. (so)

_____

3. We're going to the movies. We're going to stay home. (or)

_____

4. She doesn't like her boss. She's looking for a new job. (because)

_____

5. It's a nice day. I want to stay home. (but)

_____

6. He collects stamps. He enjoys hiking. (and)

_____

7. They read Spanish. They don't speak it. (but)

_____

8. They're learning a lot. They study hard. (so)

_____

9. They're learning a lot. They'll pass the exam. (because)

_____

10. I'm going to stop writing. This is the last item in this exercise. (so)

_____

4   *MEANING • Read these conversations. Complete them with the sentences from the box plus* **and**, **but**, **or**, **so**, *or* **because**. *More than one answer is sometimes correct.*

> I'd like you to meet her   you can practice it there   I need the exercise
> do you want to eat out   I'd really like to meet her   we can go for a walk
> I'd like to eat at home   she doesn't speak French   we can speak Spanish
> ~~I signed up for a class~~

1. A: I want to learn Spanish, _so I signed up for a class._

   B: Good idea. You're going to be in Mexico, _____

2. A: Do you want to make dinner at home, _____

   B: I just bought some fresh pasta, _____

3. A: I invited Sara for dinner _____

   B: Great. She sounds very interesting, _____

4. A: After dinner we can stay here, _____

   B: I'd like to go for a walk _____

5. A: Sara speaks Spanish, _____

   B: We can speak English with her, _____

SelfTest

SECTION ONE

Circle the letter of the correct answer to complete each sentence.

EXAMPLE: Carlos _____ a student.	**A B (C) D**
(A) are (C) is	
(B) does (D) were	

1. I'll see you _____ 8:00.   **A B C D**
   (A) in   (C) up
   (B) on   (D) at

2. She took classes _____ the summer.   **A B C D**
   (A) at   (C) from
   (B) during   (D) along

3. They came _____ taxi.   **A B C D**
   (A) in   (C) by
   (B) at   (D) with

4. He was born _____ 1999.   **A B C D**
   (A) in   (C) until
   (B) at   (D) for

5. She lives _____ Sweden.   **A B C D**
   (A) in   (C) at
   (B) on   (D) to

6. Jorge sat between Enrique and _____.   **A B C D**
   (A) I   (C) my
   (B) me   (D) mine

7. _____ do you get to school?   **A B C D**
   (A) Why   (C) Where
   (B) What   (D) How

8. Please go _____. I want to hear all about it. **A B C D**
   (A) over   (C) on
   (B) up   (D) off

9. Where did you _____?   **A B C D**
   (A) run him into   (C) into him run
   (B) him run into   (D) run into him

10. The TV is too loud. Please _____.   **A B C D**
    (A) turn down it   (C) turn over it
    (B) turn it down   (D) turn it over

11. I like Sara. We _____ along really well. **A B C D**
    (A) go   (C) get
    (B) come   (D) run

12. You don't have to dress _____. You can wear jeans. **A B C D**
    (A) down   (C) over
    (B) up   (D) in

13. We went to the beach, _____ we didn't go into the water. **A B C D**
    (A) but   (C) so
    (B) or   (D) because

14. He wants to learn English, _____ he signed up for a class. **A B C D**
    (A) but   (C) so
    (B) or   (D) because

SECTION TWO

Each sentence has four underlined parts. The four underlined parts are marked A, B, C, and D. Circle the letter of the part that is NOT CORRECT.

EXAMPLE:

Carla <u>is</u> a student, but she <u>are</u> <u>not</u> in school <u>today</u>. **A (B) C D**
    A   B C   D

15. He grew <u>up</u> <u>in</u> Venezuela, but he moved <u>in</u> Columbia <u>in</u> 2002. **A B C D**
             A B   C   D

16. <u>After</u> lunch, we walked <u>through</u> <u>the market</u> and picked <u>over</u> **A B C D**
      A   B   C   D
    some presents.

17. <u>Because</u> his shoes were dirty, he <u>took off them</u>, <u>and</u> he <u>came in</u>. **A B C D**
       A   B   C   D

18. Do you want to <u>go</u> <u>out tonight</u>, <u>or</u> do you want to stay <u>in home</u>? **A B C D**
                    A   B   C   D

19. It was late, <u>because</u> I turned <u>the TV off</u>, and <u>put</u> <u>away</u> my books. **A B C D**
               A   B   C D

20. <u>On</u> Monday, he works <u>off</u> <u>at</u> the health club <u>on</u> Main Street. **A B C D**
     A   B C   D

21. We were thirsty, <u>so</u> we walked <u>through</u> the park <u>to</u> a café, **A B C D**
                 A   B   C
    sat <u>up</u>, and ordered coffee.
        D

22. We were late <u>because</u> our car broke <u>up</u>, and we had to wait **A B C D**
                A   B
    <u>until</u> a taxi showed <u>up</u>.
     C   D

23. <u>So</u> it was late<u>,</u> we got <u>on</u> a train <u>near</u> the park. **A B C D**
     A   B   C   D

24. I cleaned <u>over</u> the kitchen, <u>hung</u> up my clothes, and <u>threw</u> **A B C D**
            A   B   C
    <u>away</u> some broken dishes.
      D

25. Dan lives far <u>from</u> school, <u>so</u> he goes <u>by car</u> or <u>in the</u> train. **A B C D**
               A   B   C   D

ANSWER KEY

2. They're not here. **OR** They aren't here.
3. We're from Turkey.
4. He's not a student. **OR** He isn't a student.
5. It's a good class.
6. There's a computer on the desk.
7. I'm twenty-one years old.
8. You're a good friend.
9. I'm not tall.
10. She's not at the library. **OR** She isn't at the library.

2. is (**OR** 's), She's (**OR** She is)   6. are
3. I'm (**OR** I am), is,   7. 're (**OR** are)
   We're (**OR** We are)   8. 'm (**OR** am)
4. is (**OR** 's), He's (**OR** He is)
5. are

3

2. There are   6. There is (**OR** There's)
3. There is (**OR** There's)   7. There are
4. There are   8. There are
5. There is (**OR** There's)

4

2. He's not (**OR** He isn't) a student.
3. aren't interested in sports.
4. aren't friends.
5. I'm not an English teacher.
6. aren't interested in baseball.
7. 're not (**OR** aren't) an English student.
8. 're not (**OR** aren't) from Australia.

5

1. is (**OR** 's)
2. 's not (**OR** isn't) (**OR** is not), 's (**OR** is)
3. 's (**OR** is)
4. is (**OR** 's), 's not (**OR** isn't) (**OR** is not)
5. 's not (**OR** isn't) (**OR** is not), 's (**OR** is)
6. are
7. is (**OR** 's)
8. aren't (**OR** are not)
9. is (**OR** 's)
10. 's not (**OR** isn't) (**OR** is not), 's (**OR** is)
11. 'm not (**OR** am not)
12. 're not (**OR** aren't) (**OR** are not)

1

2. Are your friends at the library?
3. Are you afraid of dogs?
4. Is she a doctor?
5. Am I late?
6. Are we right?
7. Are they from Mexico?
8. Is he a student?
9. Are you OK?
10. Is she here?

2. No, she's not (**OR** she isn't).
3. No, they're not (**OR** they aren't).
4. Yes, he is.
5. No, he's not (**OR** he isn't).
6. No, they're not (**OR** they aren't).
7. *Answers will vary.* No, I'm not (**OR** am not).
   (**OR** Yes, I am).
8. *Answers will vary.* No, we're not (**OR** we aren't)
   (**OR** we are not).

*Answers for **A:** will vary.*
2. Where are you from?
3. Who is your teacher?
4. What are your hobbies?
5. What are you afraid of?

1. **b.** Am
   c. No, you're not (**OR** you aren't)

2. **a.** Are
   b. No, I'm not
   c. Is she
   d. Yes, she is

3. **a.** 's (**OR** is)
   b. Is
   c. Yes, it is
   d. Are
   e. No, I'm not

UNIT 3

1

2. calling
3. leaving
4. playing
5. sitting
6. having
7. getting
8. running
9. working
10. coming

2

2. We're talking on the phone.
3. They're not listening. **OR** They aren't listening.
4. She's taking the train.
5. I'm not reading.
6. You're speaking very loud.
7. He's not sleeping. **OR** He isn't sleeping.

3

2. 's talking (**OR** is talking)
3. are studying
4. is reading (**OR** 's reading)
5. 'm (**OR** am) studying
6. 're (**OR** are) sitting
7. are doing
8. 's (**OR** is) raining
9. 'm (**OR** am) getting
10. are leaving

4

2. 's not (**OR** isn't) studying
3. aren't leaving
4. 'm not calling
5. 's not (**OR** isn't) taking
6. 's not (**OR** isn't) drinking
7. 's not (**OR** isn't) listening
8. 's not (**OR** isn't) going

5

2. 's taking (**OR** is taking)
3. 's (**OR** is) raining
4. are talking
5. is (**OR** 's) sitting
6. 's not (**OR** isn't) (**OR** is not) sleeping
7. 's not (**OR** isn't) (**OR** is not) speaking
8. 's (**OR** is) talking
9. aren't (**OR** are not) listening
10. 're (**OR** are) enjoying

UNIT 4

1

2. **Q:** Is the woman talking on the phone?
   A: No, she's not (**OR** she isn't).
3. **Q:** Is she reading?
   A: Yes, she is.
4. **Q:** Is she reading a book?
   A: No, she's not (**OR** she isn't).
5. **Q:** Is it raining?
   A: No, it's not (**OR** it isn't).
6. **Q:** Are the children watching TV?
   A: No they're not (**OR** they aren't).
7. **Q:** Are they playing?
   A: Yes, they are.
8. **Q:** Is the cat sleeping?
   A: Yes, it is.

2

2. **Q:** What is (**OR** What's) Ana reading?
   A: (She's reading) the (**OR** a) newspaper.
3. **Q:** What is (**OR** What's) the cat doing?
   A: (It's) sleeping.
4. **Q:** Where is (**OR** Where's) the cat sleeping?
   A: (It's sleeping) on the couch.
5. **Q:** Why is (**OR** Why's) the cat sleeping?
   A: (Because) it's tired.
6. **Q:** What are the children doing?
   A: (They're) playing.

3

1. **b.** Are . . . worrying
   c. Yes, I am

2. **a.** are . . . watching
   b. are . . . saying
   c. Yes, it is

3. **a.** Is . . . snowing
   b. No, it isn't (**OR** it's not)

4. **a.** are . . . looking
   b. Is . . . snowing
   c. Yes, it is
   d. are . . . doing

5. **a.** are . . . talking
   b. Is . . . meeting
   c. Yes, she is
   d. Is . . . coming
   e. No, he isn't (**OR** he's not)

SelfTest I

(Total = 100 points. Each item = 4 points.)

1. A
2. C
3. B
4. C
5. C
6. B
7. D
8. A
9. C
10. A
11. D
12. B

SECTION TWO

(Correct answers are in parentheses.)

13. B (having)
14. A (am not)
15. C (drinking)
16. C (it)
17. B (are you)
18. A (isn't OR is not)
19. B (are they)
20. C (is)
21. A (Is Lea)
22. D (?)
23. A (is drinking)
24. A (There)
25. D (they're OR they are)

UNIT 5

2. has
3. watches
4. goes
5. works
6. doesn't
7. takes
8. does
9. is
10. relaxes

2

2. go
3. study
4. goes
5. stays
6. has
7. have
8. eat

9. washes
10. does
11. read
12. relaxes

2. It always makes her nervous.
3. She usually drinks tea.
4. She sometimes adds milk and sugar.
5. Tomás usually drives to work.
6. He sometimes takes the bus.
7. He is always on time.
8. He is never late.

4

2. doesn't make Sara (OR her) nervous.
3. doesn't work in an office.
4. doesn't go to school.
5. don't live in the city.
6. don't speak English.
7. doesn't like computer games.
8. doesn't play tennis.
9. don't live near Dan.
10. don't go to the movies together.

5

2. gets
3. has
4. doesn't take
5. don't meet
6. meet
7. answers
8. doesn't have
9. writes
10. meets
11. don't meet
12. makes

UNIT 6

1

2. Does her club meet every week?
3. Does Silvio tell a lot of jokes?
4. Does Lia speak Portuguese?
5. Is Lia very funny?
6. Do Lia's friends laugh a lot?
7. Do you laugh a lot?
8. Does your club meet in the park?

2

2. **a.** Does . . . speak
   b. Yes, he does

3. **a.** Do . . . study
   b. Yes, they do

4. **a.** Do . . . belong
   b. Yes, I do

5. **a.** Does . . . meet
   b. No, it doesn't

6. **a.** Do . . . meet
   b. No, we don't

7. **a.** Does . . . cost
   b. No, it doesn't

8. **a.** Do . . . speak
   b. Yes, I do

9. **a.** Do . . . enjoy
   b. Yes, we do

3

2. When (OR How often) do they have class?
3. When do they meet?
4. How does she feel?
5. What does she wear?
6. How much does a movie ticket cost?
7. Who does he like?
8. Why does she study every day?
9. Where does she do her homework?
10. When (OR What time) does she go home?

UNIT 7

1

1. **b.** Do
   c. want

2. **a.** are
   b. doing
   c. 'm looking
   d. Do
   e. see

3. **a.** 'm
   b. Do
   c. want

4. **a.** are
   b. cooking
   c. smells
   d. Do
   e. want
   f. tastes

5. **a.** Do
   b. have
   c. need
   d. think

6. **a.** Do
   b. like
   c. love
   d. want

7. **a.** are
   b. listening
   c. sounds
   d. 's singing
   e. 're

8. **a.** 'm going
   b. Do
   c. need
   d. do
   e. mean
   f. have
   g. don't

2

1. **b.** 'm watching
   c. Is
   d. don't know
   e. looks
   f. are . . . speaking
   g. 'm trying

2. **a.** smells
   b. 'm making
   c. Do . . . want
   d. 'm drinking

3. **a.** does . . . mean
   b. don't know
   c. Do . . . have
   d. 'm looking
   e. don't understand

3

2. is
3. 's not (OR isn't) (OR is not) watching
4. 's (OR is) looking
5. thinks
6. 're (OR are)
7. doesn't (OR does not) see
8. is (OR 's) ringing
9. hears
10. 's not (OR isn't) (OR is not) answering
11. wants

UNIT 8

1

2. watches
3. doesn't (OR does not) watch
4. is (OR 's) describing
5. is (OR 's) reporting
6. doesn't (OR does not) work
7. reports
8. is starting
9. run
10. watch
11. don't (OR do not) enjoy
12. is ending
13. are crossing
14. doesn't (OR does not) want
15. 's (OR is) turning

2

2. a. are . . . doing
   b. 'm reading
3. a. want
   b. 'm doing
   c. need
4. a. does . . . go
   b. spends
5. a. Do . . . know
   b. have
   c. Do . . . want

3

2. Q: Does he usually exercise at 7:00?
   A: No, he doesn't.
3. Q: does he usually exercise?
   A: At 7:30.
4. Q: Is he taking the bus now?
   A: No, he isn't (OR he's not).
5. Q: does he report the morning news?
   A: At 9:00.
6. Q: Is he meeting with Carlos now?
   A: Yes, he is.
7. Q: Does he usually report the news at 11:00?
   A: No, he doesn't.
8. Q: Is he eating lunch now?
   A: Yes, he is.

UNIT 9

1

3. Don't come here.
4. Don't use a pen.
5. Turn right.
6. Don't close the window.
7. Don't help your partner.
8. Come early.

9. Don't push the button.
10. Park here.
11. Don't use your dictionary.
12. Ask a classmate.

2

2. look
3. Don't read
4. think
5. answer
6. Don't write
7. Tell
8. read
9. do
10. don't use
11. Use
12. check

3

2. Don't touch
3. come
4. Don't be
5. Read
6. help
7. Don't drink
8. don't call
9. Taste
10. Don't park
11. Take
12. Don't open

4

2. Go
3. Turn, Don't turn
4. Stay
5. Make
6. Don't make
7. turn
8. Be, Don't pass
9. Park

SelfTest II
(Total = 100 points. Each item = 4 points.)

SECTION ONE

1. C
2. A
3. C
4. D
5. B
6. D
7. C
8. B
9. C
10. A
11. D
12. C
13. B
14. A
15. A

(Correct answers are in parentheses.)

16. C (go)
17. B (*delete* you)
18. C (don't)
19. A (don't)
20. B (come)
21. A (doesn't)
22. A (He never)
23. A (I don't)
24. D (don't)
25. C (sometimes works)

UNIT 10

1

2. was
3. was
4. were
5. was
6. was
7. were
8. was

2

2. weren't
3. weren't
4. wasn't
5. wasn't
6. weren't
7. wasn't
8. wasn't

3

2. There was
3. There were
4. There were
5. There were
6. There was
7. There were
8. There was

4

2. Was; No, he wasn't
3. Was; No, it wasn't
4. Was; Yes, it was
5. Were; No, they weren't
6. Was; No, he wasn't
7. Was; Yes, it was

5

2. Who was with you?
3. How long was the movie?
4. When (OR What time) was it over?
5. Where was the movie?
6. How much were the tickets?
7. What was it about?
8. How was it?

UNIT 11

1

2. worked
3. liked
4. studied
5. smelled
6. hugged
7. wanted
8. hated
9. married
10. helped
11. stopped
12. tried
13. lived
14. arrived
15. hurried
16. played

2

2. wanted
3. changed
4. started
5. painted
6. studied
7. showed
8. loved, loved
9. married
10. separated, married, stayed
11. died

3

2. didn't study very hard.
3. didn't hurry to school every day.
4. didn't always arrive early.
5. didn't start at 8:00.
6. didn't paint beautiful pictures.
7. didn't work a lot.
8. didn't like painting.
9. didn't use bright colors.
10. didn't try new things.
11. didn't worry about his grades.
12. didn't work late every day.

4

2. He didn't study in England. He studied in Norway and France.
3. He didn't paint *City Night*. He painted *The Scream*.
4. He didn't die in 1863. He died in 1944.
5. He didn't paint *The Scream*. He painted *Starry Night*.
6. He didn't live in Norway. He lived in the Netherlands, Belgium, and France.
7. He didn't move to Italy and Spain. He moved to Belgium and France.
8. He didn't die at the age of 67. He died at the age of 37.
9. She didn't live in Canada. She lived in the United States.
10. She didn't study in France. She studied in the United States.
11. She didn't paint *Starry Night*. She painted *City Night*.
12. She didn't live a short life. She lived a long life.

UNIT 12

2. leave	**11.** did
3. went	**12.** meet
4. was	**13.** saw
5. come	**14.** feel
6. began	**15.** heard
7. was	**16.** found
8. had	**17.** lose
9. buy	**18.** taught
10. got	

2. Enrique went to the movies yesterday.
3. The Botteros were here yesterday.
4. Class 202 had a test yesterday.
5. Chen-Lu got a new computer yesterday.
6. Tomás made dinner yesterday.
7. Jason did the homework yesterday.
8. Mr. Thompson read the newspaper yesterday.

2. didn't leave yesterday.
3. didn't know the captain.
4. didn't see a movie.
5. didn't sleep in a hotel.
6. wasn't in Spain.
7. didn't take the train.
8. didn't spend a lot of money.
9. didn't meet interesting people.
10. didn't have a good time.

4

1. began	**5.** was, cost
2. didn't leave, left	**6.** went, didn't go
3. didn't take, took	**7.** saw, didn't see
4. didn't have, had	**8.** ate, didn't eat

UNIT 13

2. Did he fly there on Monday too?
3. Did he stay at a hotel too?
4. Did he eat dinner there too?
5. Did he go on a tour too?
6. Did he see the Pyramids too?
7. Did he meet a lot of interesting people too?
8. Did he send Kishana a postcard too?

9. Did he have a great time too?
10. Did he come home yesterday too?

2. Yes, I did	**6.** Yes, she did
3. No, I didn't	**7.** Yes, we did
4. Yes, they did	**8.** Yes, we did
5. No, he didn't	

3

2. Where did they fly?
3. Why did they go there?
4. When did they leave? OR What time did they leave?
5. Where did she stay?
6. How much did the trip cost?
7. Who did he visit?
8. What did they eat every day?
9. When were they there?
10. What did they wear?

4

2. Did . . . take; No, they didn't
3. did . . . travel; By plane
4. did . . . leave; 8:15
5. Did . . . leave; Yes, they did
6. Did . . . go; No, she didn't
7. did . . . have; Two
8. Did . . . have; No, she didn't
9. Did . . . take; Yes, he did
10. Did . . . seem; Yes, they did

SelfTest III
(Total = 100 points. Each item = 4 points.)

SECTION ONE

1. C	**9.** B
2. A	**10.** D
3. B	**11.** B
4. C	**12.** C
5. B	**13.** B
6. D	**14.** A
7. A	**15.** A
8. C	

SECTION TWO
(Correct answers are in parentheses.)

16. D (fly)	**21.** D (?)
17. D (walked)	**22.** C (didn't)
18. B (have)	**23.** A (was)
19. B (go)	**24.** B (was she)
20. B (did Tom)	**25.** C (take)

UNIT 14

1

2. We're not going to hurry. **OR** We aren't going to hurry.
3. It's going to rain.
4. You're going to be late.
5. She's not going to like it. **OR** She isn't going to like it.
6. He's going to call you.
7. They're going to fly.
8. I'm not going to stay.
9. We're going to study.
10. It's not going to be hard. **OR** It isn't going to be hard.

2

2. 're going to go
3. 's not (**OR** isn't) going to buy
4. is (**OR** 's) going to give
5. 's going to rain
6. 's not (**OR** isn't) going to be
7. 's not (**OR** isn't) going to take
8. 're going to be
9. 'm going to take
10. is (**OR** 's) going to start
11. isn't (**OR** 's not) going to arrive
12. are going to meet

3

2. Is . . . going to rain; No, it's not (**OR** it isn't)
3. Is . . . going to make; Yes, he is
4. Are . . . going to be; No, we're not (**OR** we aren't)
5. Am . . . going to need; Yes, you are
6. Are . . . going to look; No, I'm not

4

2. How many people are going to be there?
3. Where is (**OR** Where's) it going to be?
4. What is (**OR** What's) she going to buy?
5. How much (**OR** What) is it going to cost?
6. Who is (**OR** Who's) going to speak?
7. When is (**OR** When's) (**OR** What time is) (**OR** What time's) it going to end?
8. Why is (**OR** Why's) he going to leave early?

UNIT 15

1

2. It'll be nice.
3. It won't rain.
4. They'll come with us.
5. He won't be late.
6. She'll drive him here.
7. You'll like them.
8. We'll have a good time.

2

2. 'll (**OR** will) be
3. 'll (**OR** will) help
4. won't (**OR** will not) answer
5. won't (**OR** will not) give
6. 'll (**OR** will) try
7. won't (**OR** will not) be
8. 'll (**OR** will) be
9. 'll (**OR** will) see
10. will call
11. won't (**OR** will not) speak
12. won't (**OR** will not) give
13. 'll (**OR** will) ask
14. won't (**OR** will not) quit

3

2. Will . . . see; No, I won't
3. Will . . . be; Yes, she will
4. Will . . . come; No, he won't
5. Will . . . be; No it won't
6. Will . . . like; Yes, they will
7. Will . . . get; Yes, it will

4

2. **A:** Who will you invite?
   B: My classmates.
3. **A:** How many people will come?
   B: Fifteen.
4. **A:** When will the guests arrive?
   B: At 8:00.
5. **A:** What will you wear?
   B: Jeans.
6. **A:** How will Enrique get to the party?
   B: By train.
7. **A:** How much soda will you buy?
   B: Twenty bottles.
8. **A:** Where will you buy it?
   B: At the supermarket.

SelfTest IV

(*Total = 100 points. Each item = 4 points.*)

1. A	**7.** C
2. A	**8.** C
3. D	**9.** A
4. B	**10.** C
5. D	**11.** C
6. B	**12.** C

SECTION TWO

(*Correct answers are in parentheses.*)

13. B (going to have)
14. A (is he)
15. D (tomorrow night)
16. A (pick)
17. B (are they)
18. A (Where is he)
19. B (your friends going to)
20. A (won't **OR** will not)
21. C (going to do)
22. B (*delete* going to)
23. D (have)
24. A (Are)
25. D (?)

UNIT 16

One Object: 2, 4, 8
Two Objects: 3, 5, 6, 7

2. She bought a stamp at the post office.
3. She mailed the letter yesterday.
4. Her friend received it on Tuesday.
5. She read it at school.
6. She didn't understand the letter.
7. She didn't call her friend.
8. She e-mailed her friend the next day.

2. him a cake.
3. her new CD, me.
4. a map, them.
5. us chocolate.
6. you my notes.

3. I read my little brother the story.
4. They sold Mr. and Mrs. Hampton the house.
5. She showed her new jacket to me.
6. I handed the teacher my report.
7. He sold his bike to Jason.
8. Jason told a story to him.

UNIT 17

2. When (**OR** What time) does his favorite show begin?
3. Why does he watch it?
4. Who does he like?
5. How many questions did he answer last night?
6. What does he always eat during the show?
7. When (**OR** What time) does the show end?
8. Who does he call after the show?

2. How many people saw it?
3. Who liked it?
4. Who knew a lot of the answers?
5. What happened?
6. Who won a lot of money?
7. Who gave the money to a hospital?
8. How many people called the show?

2. What did you watch?
3. Where did you go after the program?
4. Who went with you?
5. How many whole pizzas did you eat?
6. How much did it cost?
7. When (**OR** What time) did you go home?
8. Why did you go home?

2. A game show.
3. To an Italian restaurant.
4. Malov's sister.
5. Three.
6. $40.
7. 10:00 P.M.
8. Malov felt sick.

SelfTest V

(Total = 100 points. Each item = 4 points.)

SECTION ONE

1.	B	7.	A
2.	A	8.	A
3.	D	9.	A
4.	B	10.	C
5.	A	11.	A
6.	C	12.	A

SECTION TWO

(Correct answers are in parentheses.)

13. B (did you)
14. C (a book to the teacher **OR** the teacher a book)
15. B (did you mail)
16. A (saw the movie)
17. C (saw)
18. B (to you)
19. B (go to the beach)
20. B (did you see **OR** saw you)
21. D (?)
22. B (did you read)
23. B (did they)
24. B (*delete* did)
25. D (in the store *goes after* help)

UNIT 18

1

2.	e	6.	c
3.	a	7.	f
4.	d	8.	b
5.	g		

2

1. I will be at my brother's house in ~~s~~eoul *(S)* on ~~s~~unday *(S)*, ~~n~~ovember *(N)* 9th.
2. My friend ~~c~~armen *(C)* is studying ~~f~~rench *(F)* in ~~p~~aris *(P)*.
3. Dave works for ~~s~~ony *(S)* records as an accountant.
4. Jorge is a chef at a ~~m~~exican *(M)* restaurant in ~~t~~exas *(T)*.
5. Lola lives at 2342 ~~m~~ain *(M)* ~~s~~treet *(S)* in ~~l~~ondon *(L)*.

3

3.	countries	9.	boxes
4.	men	10.	foot
5.	X	11.	person
6.	children	12.	X
7.	woman	13.	books
8.	knives	14.	houses

4

2. people, prefer
3. catalog, is
4. store, is
5. customer, has
6. are, stores
7. store, has
8. store, sells
9. shoes, look
10. women, shop, men
11. earrings, are
12. pairs, earrings, are

5

I hate to shop for clothes. I don't like crowded ~~Stores~~ *(stores)*. In large stores, ~~saleswoman~~ *(saleswomen)* and salesmen ~~is~~ *(are)* too busy. In small stores, ~~salespeoples~~ *(salespeople)* are "too helpful": They don't leave you alone. In *all* ~~store~~ *(stores)*, the dressing rooms ~~is~~ *(are)* uncomfortable.

Clothes ~~is~~ *(are)* important, but I don't buy ~~it~~ *(them)* in stores because ~~Time~~ *(time)* is important too. I shop online. There ~~is~~ *(are)* many good things about online stores. First of all, they are always open: twenty-four ~~hour~~ *(hours)* a day, seven ~~day~~ *(days)* a week. You can shop on a ~~sunday~~ *(Sunday)* or on a holiday. It's an easy and fast ~~ways~~ *(way)* to shop. I finish my order with just a few ~~click~~ *(clicks)* of my computer mouse, and my order arrives in just a few ~~day~~ *(days)*. Best of all, it's comfortable. I can try on that new pair of ~~jean~~ *(jeans)* in my own home.

So, do you really hate to shop too? Stay home! No more standing on those long ~~line~~ *(lines)*! Shop online! Your order is just one ~~clicks~~ *(click)* away!

UNIT 19

Count Nouns: teacher, pen, spoon, number, book
Non-Count Nouns: Spanish, salt, soup, milk, health, homework

2. milk
3. books
4. homework
5. soup
6. health
7. salt
8. pen
9. numbers
10. teachers
11. Spanish
12. spoons

3

2. 4 bars of soap
3. 2 cans of soup
4. 1 loaf of bread
5. 2 pounds of potatoes
6. 2 bottles of water

4

3. milk
4. glasses
5. milk
6. cookies
7. cookies
8. are
9. recipe
10. is
11. tastes
12. nuts
13. are
14. chocolate
15. comes
16. nuts
17. oven
18. sugar
19. butter
20. goes
21. eggs

UNIT 20

1

2. an
3. an
4. an
5. a
6. an
7. a
8. a
9. a
10. a
11. an
12. a
13. an
14. an
15. an
16. a

2

2. An
3. The
4. a
5. the
6. a
7. an
8. a, a
9. a
10. the
11. The
12. a
13. the
14. The
15. The, the
16. The, the
17. The, the
18. the, The

3

2. a
3. an
4. The
5. a
6. a
7. the
8. the
9. the
10. The
11. The
12. the
13. a
14. a
15. the
16. a
17. The
18. the
19. the

4

                            The
Find X̶ Home of Your Dreams
                        a   *A*
Are you looking for ~~the~~ new home? ~~The~~ real estate
                                                        The
agent can help you find the home of your dreams. ~~A~~ right
agent can save you a lot of time—and money.

Describe your dream home, and your agent will help
                                    the
you from the beginning to the ~~an~~ end: from looking at
                    the   *the*
your home for ~~a~~ first time, to finding ~~a~~ best moving
                            the
company. We are ~~a~~ largest real estate agency in the
                                            the
country. We can help you the find ~~a~~ best house for you.

Call us at 555-HOME. We have more than 100 agents.
An
~~The~~ agent will be happy to help you.

136

UNIT 21

1

2. This coffee is very strong.
3. These students study hard.
4. This music is loud.
5. He sings them in a lot of concerts.
6. I like these songs.

2

1. clothes
2. The clothes, the salespeople
3. jeans, skirts
4. The T-Shirts, The prices
5. The music, the cafeteria
6. the coffee, coffee
7. concerts, tickets
8. the concert, the tickets

3

2. the, —
3. —, —, the, the
4. —, —, —
5. The, the
6. —, —
7. —, the
8. the, the
9. —, the, the, —, the
10. —, the, the
11. —
12. The, the

UNIT 22

1

2. some
3. some
4. any
5. some
6. some
7. some
8. any
9. some
10. any, some
11. any
12. some
13. any

2

3. any bananas
4. any homework
5. some tests
6. any coffee
7. some tea
8. some ice cream
9. some chocolate ice cream
10. any nuts

3

2. any furniture
3. any snow
4. some cookies
5. any . . . photos
6. any electricity
7. some students
8. any . . . cups

4

2. some . . . (running) shoes
3. some letters
4. any stamps
5. any . . . games
6. some videos **OR** movies
7. some eggs
8. any chicken
9. (any) carrots

UNIT 23

1

Many: friends, people, tests, CDs, movies
Much: water, time, work, music
A Few: friends, people, tests, CDs, movies
A Little: water, time, work, music
A Lot of: water, time, friends, people, work, tests, music, CDs, movies

2

2. much
3. many
4. a lot of
5. many
6. a few
7. a little
8. a few
9. many
10. a few
11. many
12. many
13. Many
14. a lot
15. a lot of

3

2. a few (**OR** aren't many)
3. a lot of (**OR** many)
4. a few (**OR** aren't many)
5. a few (**OR** aren't many)
6. a little (**OR** isn't much)
7. a lot of
8. a few (**OR** aren't many)
9. a few (**OR** aren't many)
10. a lot of

4

2. How many, many (**OR** a lot of)
3. How many, a few, much (**OR** a lot of)
4. How much, a lot
5. How many, a lot of (**OR** many)
6. How much, a little
7. How much, A lot
8. How many, a few

UNIT 24

1

2. there is (**OR** there's)
3. There will be
4. There are
5. There will be
6. There was
7. There were
8. There is (**OR** There's)

2

2. There won't be
3. There isn't
4. there aren't
5. There's **OR** There is
6. There wasn't
7. There are
8. There won't be

3

2. How much soda is there?
3. How many tables were there?
4. How many people will there be?
5. How much time will there be?

4

2. Is there any; No, there isn't (**OR** there's not).
3. Are there any; No, there aren't.
4. Are there any; Yes, there are.
5. Are there any; Yes, there are.
6. Is there any; Yes, there is.
7. Is there any; No, there isn't (**OR** there's not).
8. Is there any; Yes, there is.
9. Is there any; No, there isn't (**OR** there's not).
10. Is there any; No, there isn't (**OR** there's not).

SelfTest VI
(Total = 100 points. Each item = 4 points.)

SECTION ONE

1.	D	7.	B
2.	A	8.	C
3.	C	9.	B
4.	D	10.	D
5.	B	11.	B
6.	A	12.	A

SECTION TWO

(Correct answers are in parentheses.)

13. D (year)
14. A (women)
15. D (the movie)
16. D (coffee)
17. A (an)
18. C (Brazil)
19. C (a)
20. B (a)
21. A (is)
22. D (a lot)
23. C (shorts)
24. B (cup of tea)
25. C (a lot of **OR** many)

UNIT 25

1

SUBJECT	OBJECT
you	you
he	*him*
she	*her*
it	*it*
we	us
you	*you*
they	them

2

2. It
3. I
4. them
5. her
6. She
7. I
8. me
9. It's
10. it
11. they
12. it
13. me
14. her

3

2. They played with it.
3. He baked them.
4. She gave it to her.
5. She loved it.
6. It looked great on her.
7. Did he like it too?
8. He sat between them.
9. I sent it to her.
10. Did you give them to them?
11. She told him about it.
12. He recommended it to her.

4

2. It	18. I
3. you	19. you
4. I	20. us
5. it	21. it
6. me	22. It
7. you	23. them
8. you	24. I
9. it	25. they
10. It	26. I
11. I	27. her
12. you	28. I
13. I	29. me
14. it	30. her
15. It	31. I
16. you	32. you
17. you	

UNIT 26

1

This is _____ hat.	This hat is _____.
her	his
his	mine
the man's	the man's
Marta's	yours
my	Marta's
their	the girls'
the girls'	theirs
your	ours

2

2. b	7. b
3. a	8. a
4. b	9. b
5. b	10. a
6. b	

3

2. That's not my hat
3. My hat isn't white
4. That's Natalie's hat
5. Is her hat white
6. It isn't hers
7. Hers is smaller
8. Whose is this
9. That's my mother's hat

4

1. **b.** My
   c. Todd's
   d. His OR Todd's
2. **a.** yours
   b. mine
3. **a.** hers OR Mai's
   b. her OR Mai's
4. **a.** theirs OR Henri and Lisa's
   b. our
   c. ours

UNIT 27

1

2. This	6. This
3. that	7. This
4. This	8. That
5. this, this	

2

2. those
3. those
4. Those
5. these
6. These
7. Those
8. These

1. b. These

2. a. These
   b. This

3. a. these
   b. that

4. a. This
   b. This
   c. This

5. a. those
   b. These

6. a. That
   b. That

7. a. Those
   b. these

8. a. that
   b. those

9. a. This
   b. These
   c. This

10. a. that
   b. that

2. Is that; Yes, it is
3. Are these; Yes, they are
4. Is this; Yes, it is
5. Are those; Yes, they are
6. Is this; Yes, it is

UNIT 28

1

2. ones
3. ones
4. one
5. ones
6. one

2

2. Which one?
3. Which one?
4. Which ones?
5. Which ones?
6. Which one?

3

1. b. one

2. a. one
   b. one

3. a. ones
   b. ones
   c. ones
   d. ones
   e. one

4. a. ones   **e.** one
   b. ones   **f.** one
   c. ones   **g.** one
   d. one   **h.** ones

I ordered three sweaters through your online catalog—a gray *one* ~~ones~~ and two black *ones* ~~one~~. The black ones are fine, but the gray *one* ~~ones~~ is too small. All three say size "medium." I'd like to return the gray *one* ~~ones~~ and get another black *one* ~~ones~~. There are two different return forms on your Website. Which *one* ~~ones~~ should I use?

SelfTest VII
(Total = 100 points. Each item = 4 points.)

SECTION ONE

1. B   **8.** B
2. A   **9.** C
3. C   **10.** D
4. C   **11.** C
5. B   **12.** B
6. B   **13.** D
7. C

SECTION TWO
(Correct answers are in parentheses.)

14. C (that)   **20.** C (one)
15. D (one)   **21.** C (one)
16. B (cousin)   **22.** D (it)
17. D (Megan's)   **23.** C (brother's)
18. B (your)   **24.** A (Which)
19. C (those)   **25.** D (some)

140

UNIT 29

1

2.	g	6.	b
3.	d	7.	f
4.	c	8.	a
5.	i	9.	e

2

2. It has a big garden.
3. There's a sunny kitchen.
4. The living room looks comfortable.
5. The bedroom seems large.
6. They have a nice office.
7. Their cat is cute.
8. She's a friendly cat.

3

2. beach, crowded
3. cool, water
4. large, mall
5. new, clothes
6. beautiful, sweater
7. expensive
8. Mexican, student
9. English, class
10. teacher, good

4

I like my ~~class English~~ _English class_. The teacher is very good,
and the students ~~friendly are~~ _are friendly_. Our classroom is very
pleasant too. It's not a ~~room big~~ _big room_, but it's sunny and has
~~comfortables~~ _comfortable_ chairs. There's only one problem—it
sometimes gets ~~hotly~~ _hot_. We can't open the windows because
then it's noisy.

Tomorrow we are going on a class trip. I hope it's a
~~day hot~~ _hot day_ because we're going to the beach. There are some
~~beautifuls~~ _beautiful_ beaches near the school. I can wear my new
swimsuit. Janna says the water is great. That's good
news. I want to go swimming!

UNIT 30

1

2. a
3. c
4. b
5. a
6. b

2

2. as old as
3. not as old as
4. not as tall as
5. as tall as
6. not as short as
7. not as heavy as
8. not as heavy as
9. not as good as
10. as good as

3

2. isn't (OR is not) as expensive
3. isn't (OR is not) as tall as
4. isn't (OR is not) as busy
5. aren't (OR are not) as good
6. is as big as
7. isn't (OR is not) as old
8. isn't (OR is not) as athletic
9. 's (OR is) as popular as
10. 's (OR is) as happy as

UNIT 31

1

2.	bigger	9.	more popular
3.	nicer	10.	shorter
4.	happier	11.	prettier
5.	more interesting	12.	worse
6.	better	13.	more difficult
7.	stronger	14.	farther
8.	more intelligent		

2

2. more expensive than
3. lighter than
4. heavier than
5. better than
6. worse than
7. shorter than
8. longer than

2. more expensive than
3. more athletic
4. taller
5. stronger than
6. more difficult
7. more successful than
8. farther
9. happier
10. easier

2. The plane is faster than the train.
3. The train is more expensive than the bus.
4. A monkey is more intelligent than a dog.
5. My grades are better than your grades.
6. Tara is heavier than her sister.
7. Calculus is more difficult than algebra.
8. Dina is happier than her brother.
9. The bookstore is farther than the café.
10. The movie is worse than the book.
11. Mexico City is hotter than Paris.
12. Luis is funnier than Enrique.

UNIT 32

2. the biggest
3. the funniest
4. the most interesting
5. the hottest
6. the best
7. the most amazing
8. the most wonderful
9. the spiciest
10. the fattest
11. the coldest
12. the worst
13. the farthest
14. the nicest
15. the most important
16. the easiest

2. Y, the most expensive
3. Z, the saltiest
4. X, the spiciest
5. Z, the sweetest
6. Y, the thickest
7. X, the thinnest
8. Z, the chunkiest
9. Z, the best
10. the most delicious

1. the most expensive
2. the most popular, the longest
3. the oldest, the darkest
4. the worst, the cheapest
5. the funniest, the most delicious

Last night I ate at the Florentine Grill. In a city with more than 100 restaurants, this is the ~~more~~ *most* beautiful restaurant in town. It's also the ~~expensivest~~ *most expensive*. I was with a group of four people, and we each ordered something different. The chicken with mushrooms and cream was definitely the ~~deliciousest~~ *most delicious*. The ~~more~~ *most* unusual dish was fish in a nut sauce. Very interesting. My wife likes spicy food. Her spaghetti arrabiatta (in a hot pepper sauce) was the ~~most~~ hottest dish. (She almost couldn't eat it.) My steak was good, but not the ~~better~~ *best*. Desserts were terrific. They make the ~~good~~ *best* chocolate soufflé in the world!

I recommend the Florentine Grill for a special event. Be sure to make a reservation. This is one of the ~~popularest~~ *most popular* restaurants in town.

UNIT 33

2. My apartment is too cold.
3. Her grades are good enough.
4. His car is not very fast.
5. The coffee is not too strong.
6. Our apartment is not cheap enough.
7. The music is too loud.
8. The soup is salty enough.

2.	b	7.	b
3.	b	8.	a
4.	b	9.	c
5.	c	10.	c
6.	b		

3

2. light enough
3. big enough
4. too old
5. hot enough
6. warm enough
7. too difficult
8. too loud
9. comfortable enough
10. too dark
11. too tired
12. well enough
13. cheap enough
14. too young

4

2. too high **OR** very high
3. big enough **OR** very big
4. very dirty **OR** too dirty
5. very comfortable **OR** comfortable enough
6. very healthy **OR** healthy enough
7. very neat **OR** neat enough
8. too low **OR** very low
9. too small **OR** very small
10. warm enough **OR** very warm

UNIT 34

1

2. beautiful
3. well
4. quickly
5. horrible
6. fast
7. easily
8. friendly
9. fantastically
10. hard
11. happily
12. late

2

2. a
3. a
4. a
5. a
6. b
7. a
8. b
9. b
10. a

3

1. well
2. softly, weak
3. beautiful, well
4. hard, good
5. close, hard
6. early, late
7. quickly, slowly

4

Last night I went to my first baseball game! I had a
~~wonderfully~~ *wonderful* time. We had great seats, and I could see
very ~~good~~ *well*. Jon knows the game ~~perfect~~ *perfectly*, and he explained
the rules very clearly.

Sometimes the game moves ~~slow~~ *slowly*. Not much happens.
But then all at once it becomes exciting.

The other team's pitcher (the pitcher throws the
ball) threw the ball ~~hardly~~ *hard* and fast. One time the ball hit
the batter (the batter usually hits *the ball*!). That can be
dangerous, because the ball is very hard and it moves
very ~~fastly~~ *fast*. But it didn't hurt him ~~bad~~ *badly*, and he could stay
in the game. That was lucky for our team. The next time
he was at bat, he hit the ball hard and far. The ball flew
~~quick~~ *quickly* out of the field. That's called a "home run." The
crowd stood up and screamed ~~loud~~ *loudly*. They were really
~~happily~~ *happy*. The final score was 10 to 3. Our team won ~~easy~~ *easily*.

The game is just part of the event. In addition, we
ate some typical "ball park" food—hot dogs (a type of
sausage) and French fries. It tasted ~~greatly~~ *great* with some
cold soda.

The day was ~~perfectly~~ *perfect*. I had a really great time, and
I am looking forward to the next game.

SelfTest VIII
(Total = 100 points. Each item = 4 points.)

SECTION ONE

1. A
2. B
3. C
4. B
5. D
6. C
7. B
8. C
9. A
10. B

SECTION TWO
(Correct answers are in parentheses.)

11. B (the most)
12. D (big enough)
13. D (late)
14. D (terrible)
15. C (*delete* as)
16. B (easy)

17. A (the worst)
18. D (easily)
19. B (beautiful)
20. B (best)
21. C (heavy)
22. B (cheaper)
23. A (worst)
24. C (nervous)
25. C (too big)

Unit 35

2. couldn't talk, can talk
3. couldn't give, can't give
4. can write, could write
5. couldn't write, can write
6. can read, could read
7. couldn't read, can read
8. couldn't understand, can understand
9. couldn't understand, can't understand
10. can, could

2. Could your brother drive last year?; No, he couldn't
3. Could your sister understand the movie last night?; Yes, she could
4. Can your mother still run fast?; Yes, she can
5. Could she swim as a child?; No, she couldn't; can't
6. Can your brother win a race now?; No, he can't

3

2. How many hours (OR How long) could his sister play tennis?
3. How high could his brother jump?
4. How many books (a week) can you read?
5. What could Ana play (as a child)?
6. How much ice cream can you eat (at one time)?
7. Where could your little sister fall asleep (as a child)?

Unit 36

1

2. Why doesn't he
3. Why don't we
4. Why don't you
5. Why doesn't she
6. Why don't I
7. Why don't they
8. Why don't you

2. Let's hurry
3. Let's not take
4. Let's ask
5. Let's not have
6. Let's go
7. Let's not stay
8. Let's watch

2. How about getting
3. How about going
4. How about inviting
5. How about riding
6. How about studying
7. How about putting
8. How about talking

1. Let's make
2. Why don't you ask
3. Let's watch, Let's not watch
4. Why don't we make, Let's invite
5. Why doesn't she join
6. Let's go, Why don't we try
7. Let's not go, Let's stay
8. Let's clean, Why don't we start

Unit 37

1

2. Can you open
3. Would you explain
4. Will you hurry
5. Could you carry
6. Can you get
7. Would you give
8. Will you call

2. Will you please call me?
3. Can you please help me?
4. Would you please be quiet?
5. Could you please close the door?
6. Can you please wait?
7. Could you please wash the dishes?
8. Would you please come early?

3

2. Of course
3. Sorry, I can't
4. Sure
5. No problem
6. No, I can't

4

2. Will (**OR** Would) (**OR** Can) (**OR** Could) you
   e-mail; Of course (**OR** Certainly) (**OR** Sure)
   (**OR** No problem)
3. Will (**OR** Would) (**OR** Can) (**OR** Could) you call;
   Of course (**OR** Certainly) (**OR** Sure) (**OR** No
   problem)
4. Will (**OR** Would) (**OR** Can) (**OR** Could) you type;
   Sorry, I can't
5. Will (**OR** Would) (**OR** Can) (**OR** Could) you make
   copies; Of course (**OR** Certainly) (**OR** Sure) (**OR** No
   problem)
6. Will (**OR** Would) (**OR** Can) (**OR** Could) you buy; Of
   course (**OR** Certainly) (**OR** Sure) (**OR** No problem)
7. Will (**OR** Would) (**OR** Can) (**OR** Could) you pay;
   Of course (**OR** Certainly) (**OR** Sure) (**OR** No problem)

UNIT 38

1

2. we swim in the lake?
3. she use the phone?
4. I take the test now?
5. Henri borrow the car?
6. I take your picture?
7. I use my cell phone?
8. we leave now?

2

2. Can we please change our seats?
3. Could I please ask a question?
4. Can I please leave now?
5. Could I please open the window?
6. May we please sit here?

3

2. Yes, you can
3. No, you may not
4. No, you can't
5. Sure

4

3. Can we go
4. Sorry, you can't
5. May I use
6. Of course **OR** Certainly **OR** Sure **OR** No problem
7. Could I listen
8. Of course **OR** Certainly **OR** Sure **OR** No problem
9. May I (**OR** we) use
10. Sorry, you can't
11. Could I (**OR** we) have
12. Of course **OR** Certainly **OR** Sure
    OR No problem

SelfTest IX

(Total = 100 points. Each item = 4 points.)

SECTION ONE

1. A		**6.**	B
2. A		**7.**	D
3. B		**8.**	C
4. A		**9.**	A
5. C		**10.**	B

SECTION TWO

(Correct answers are in parentheses.)

11. B (please open)
12. A (Why don't)
13. D (read)
14. B (have a party)
15. B (not)
16. C (don't we)
17. A (May I please)
18. D (could/would/can/will you)
19. C (cannot **OR** can't)
20. C (could you)
21. B (please lend)
22. A (Would/Could/Will/Would)
23. A (Could you)
24. C (couldn't)
25. C (swim)

UNIT 39

1

2. He'd like to go to the movies.
3. They'd like to take a break.
4. She'd like to have a cup of coffee.
5. I'd like to finish this exercise.
6. We'd like to leave now.

2. 'd rather not go
3. 'd rather take
4. 'd rather not stay
5. 'd rather shop
6. 'd rather not buy
7. 'd rather send
8. 'd rather not go
9. 'd rather wear
10. 'd rather not run

2. Would you like to fly?
4. Would you rather take
5. No, I wouldn't **OR** I'd rather not
6. Would you rather rent
7. No, I wouldn't **OR** I'd rather not
8. Would you like to travel
9. No, I wouldn't **OR** I'd rather not

Steve Parker completed the transportation survey and answered some interview questions. According to Parker, for a business trip he'd always like to fly. He'd ~~not rather~~ rather not take the train or the bus. One of the questions was: ~~You would~~ Would you rather drive or take the train? ~~He~~ He'd rather drive. He really hates the bus. He'd rather not ~~takes~~ take it. In fact, he said, "I'd rather ~~walking~~ walk!"

UNIT 40

Definitely: 3, 6, 7
Possibly: 2, 4, 5, 8

2. might not buy
3. could get
4. might go
5. couldn't
6. might call
7. might not go
8. may return
9. might not be
10. might leave
11. may have
12. might not go

3. Is he going to clean the living room?; He might.
4. Is he going to bake a cake?; Yes, he is.
5. Is he going to call Lydia?; He might.
6. Is he going to do English homework?; Yes, he is.
7. Is he going to e-mail Zlatan?; Yes, he is.
8. Is he going to do laundry?; He might not.

Hi, Elissa—I'm going to go to the library, and I might ~~no~~ not be home before 6:00. I may ~~not~~ go to the supermarket on the way home. Do we need anything? Tania is going to come to dinner, but Anton ~~mayn't~~ may not. He doesn't feel well. ~~May you~~ Are you going to make tacos for dinner? You know, it might be a good idea. It's easy, and everyone loves them. Oh, and please remember to close the window. It might ~~rains~~ rain. Call me. I have my cell with me.—Vania

UNIT 41

2. shouldn't wait
3. should ask
4. should work
5. shouldn't go
6. should eat
7. shouldn't be
8. should do

2

2. You ought to learn some Portuguese before your trip.
3. You ought to spend some time in Lisbon.
4. You should wear comfortable shoes.
5. You shouldn't forget to take a dictionary.
6. You ought to try the seafood.
7. You shouldn't visit only Lisbon.

3

1. Yes, you should
2. Should . . . go; No, you shouldn't
3. Should . . . speak; No, you shouldn't
4. Should . . . visit; Yes, you should
5. Should . . . make; Yes, you should
6. Should . . . send; Yes, you should

4

2. When should I go?
3. Where should I go?
4. How should I go there?
5. Why should I go there?
6. How long should I go for? **OR** For how long should I go?
7. What should I buy?

UNIT 42

1

2. has to
3. doesn't have to
4. doesn't have to
5. has to
6. doesn't have to
7. has to
8. doesn't have to
9. has to
10. have to
11. don't have to
12. *Answers will vary*: have to **OR** don't have to
13. *Answers will vary*: have to **OR** don't have to

2

2. does . . . have to use
3. Does . . . have to wear
4. Do . . . have to speak
5. Do . . . have to arrive
6. Does . . . have to write
7. does . . . have to finish
8. Do . . . have to leave

3

2. must not
3. must
4. must not
5. must not
6. must
7. must
8. must

4

2. don't have to
3. must not
4. must not
5. must not
6. must not
7. don't have to
8. must not

SelfTest X
(Total = 100 points. Each item = 4 points.)

SECTION ONE

1. A
2. C
3. B
4. B
5. C
6. A
7. A
8. B
9. C
10. B
11. D
12. A
13. D

SECTION TWO
(Correct answers are in parentheses.)

14. D (have)
15. B (to stay)
16. C (rather not)
17. B (take)
18. B (ought to call)
19. A (don't have to)
20. A (has)
21. D (stay)
22. C (couldn't **OR** won't **OR** 's not going to)
23. C (should we)
24. D (send)
25. C (I'd rather)

UNIT 43

2. writing, to write
3. swimming, to swim
4. walking, to walk
5. hurrying, to hurry
6. hitting, to hit
7. moving, to move
8. exercising, to exercise

2. swimming	8. to make
3. to leave	9. buying
4. to stay	10. inviting
5. being	11. to drive
6. bringing	12. to go
7. to be	

2. not driving
3. not to stay
4. not to leave
5. not having
6. not inviting
7. not to stay
8. not swimming

4

2. to have a sandwich.
3. not going too far.
4. not to go far.
5. reading.
6. getting some ice cream.
7. eating ice cream.
8. to leave now.

UNIT 44

1

2. She went to the supermarket to buy some eggs.
3. He called Dr. Ellin to make an appointment.
4. They went to the library to study for a test.
5. She went to Mexico to learn Spanish.
6. They needed a lot of tomatoes to make spaghetti sauce.

2. She made a shopping list in order not to forget things.
3. He eats only low-fat food in order not to gain weight.
4. They spoke softly in order not to wake the baby.
5. She copies all her files onto CDs in order not to lose important information.

2. to meet
3. to practice
4. in order not to spend
5. to keep
6. To ask
7. in order not to miss
8. to do
9. To remind
10. to buy
11. To invite
12. To study

SelfTest XI
(Total = 100 points. Each item = 4 points.)

SECTION ONE

1. D	8. B
2. B	9. D
3. C	10. A
4. D	11. C
5. A	12. B
6. C	13. D
7. C	

SECTION TWO
(Correct answers are in parentheses.)

14. D (staying)
15. D (to be)
16. D (eating)
17. C (to)
18. C (not to)
19. D (to forget)
20. D (to finish)
21. D (to check)
22. B (buying)
23. A (to use)
24. C (to give)
25. D (not to take)

Unit 45

1

1. at
2. How long, until
3. at, by
4. How long, For
5. from, to, on
6. during, in, for
7. during, at
8. in, by
9. at, at, until
10. in, for

2

2. in OR during
3. During
4. at
5. after OR at
6. for
7. until OR on
8. On
9. At
10. in OR for

3

2. at
3. before
4. until
5. from, to (OR until)
6. for
7. after
8. at
9. During
10. from, to (OR until)
11. at
12. in

Unit 46

1

2. at
3. in, across from
4. near
5. on
6. in, next to
7. on
8. at
9. in
10. in
11. on
12. between, him

2

2. on, under
3. in, on
4. over
5. between
6. next to, on, on
7. in back of
8. at

3

2. in
3. on
4. at
5. between
6. over OR above
7. to the left
8. on
9. on
10. to the right
11. in
12. on
13. in OR in the middle of
14. over OR above
15. in
16. on
17. under
18. to the right of OR next to

Unit 47

1

2. through
3. from
4. to
5. along
6. toward
7. across
8. to
9. into
10. around
11. out of
12. to
13. down
14. home
15. by

2

2. by
3. on
4. over
5. in
6. along
7. toward
8. into
9. through
10. out of
11. on
12. under
13. down
14. through
15. off, up

3

Hi, Ian! This city is great. Today we went for a long
walk ~~through~~ _along_ the beautiful river. Then we walked ~~above~~ _up_
this big hill. From the top of the hill we could look ~~under~~ _over_
the red rooftops of the city's old buildings. What a
beautiful view! We were tired, so we walked ~~out of~~ _into OR to_ a café
and sat down for a cup of coffee. And that's where I am
now. I'm writing postcards, and the server just put some
little cakes ~~in~~ _on_ the table. They look delicious. After I eat
them, I'm going to take the postcards ~~toward~~ _to_ the post
office and mail them there. Then we'll go back to the
hotel. Tomorrow is our last day. I had a great time, but
I'm happy to go home.

See you soon. —M

Unit 48

1

2. g
3. a
4. j
5. h
6. d
7. e
8. c
9. f
10. b

2. along
3. up
4. up
5. into
6. out
7. along
8. on
9. up
10. back
11. together
12. out
13. up
14. down
15. up

2. When did your TV break down?
3. The students sometimes hang out together at the pizza place.
4. Sometimes it's difficult for Paulo to stay up late.
5. Please don't hang up now.
6. Sit down and relax.
7. How did that come about?
8. When will you come back?
9. Sonia dressed up for her party.
10. They kept on working until 6:00.
11. Mike was bored at school, so he dropped out.
12. I want to sign up for another language class.

UNIT 49

2. f
3. i
4. a
5. g
6. c
7. e
8. j
9. d
10. b

2

2. back
3. on
4. down
5. up
6. back
7. down
8. over

3

2. called him up
3. put it off
4. handed it in
5. turn it down
6. ask her over
7. do it over
8. talk them over

4

2. We worked it out together.
3. Please turn the volume down (**OR** turn down the volume).
4. Let's ask her over for dinner.
5. Please fill this form out (**OR** fill out this form) with a pen.
6. I'll give it back after class.
7. I always look my homework over (**OR** look over my homework) carefully before class.
8. Pick out the one (**OR** Pick the one out) you like best.

UNIT 50

2. or
3. so
4. and
5. because
6. so
7. but
8. so
9. but
10. Because

2

2. because
3. Because
4. , so
5. because
6. , so
7. because
8. because
9. because
10. , so

3

2. I'm late, so I have to hurry.
3. We're going to the movies, or we're going to stay home. **OR** We're going to stay home, or we're going to the movies.
4. She's looking for a new job because she doesn't like her boss. **OR** Because she doesn't like her boss, she's looking for a new job.
5. It's a nice day, but I want to stay home.
6. He collects stamps, and he enjoys hiking. **OR** He enjoys hiking, and he collects stamps.
7. They read Spanish, but they don't speak it.
8. They study hard, so they're learning a lot.
9. Because they're learning a lot, they'll pass the exam. **OR** They'll pass the exam because they're learning a lot.
10. This is the last item in this exercise, so I'm going to stop writing.

4

1. so you can practice it there.
2. or do you want to eat out?; so I'd like to eat at home.
3. because I'd like you to meet her.; so (**OR** and) I'd really like to meet her.
4. or we can go for a walk.; because I need the exercise.
5. but she doesn't speak French.; or we can speak Spanish.

SelfTest XII
(Total = 100 points. Each item = 4 points.)

SECTION ONE

1.	D	**9.**	D
2.	B	**10.**	B
3.	C	**11.**	C
4.	A	**12.**	B
5.	A	**13.**	A
6.	B	**14.**	C
7.	D		
8.	C		

SECTION TWO
(Correct answers are in parentheses.)

15. C (to)
16. D (out)
17. B (took them off)
18. D (at home **OR** home)
19. A (so)
20. B (out)
21. D (down)
22. B (down)
23. A (Because)
24. A (up)
25. D (by)